AIRCRAⸯ ⸯ ⸯ
Flying Accidents in Gwyⁿⸯ
1910-1990

AIRCRAFT CRASHES

Flying accidents in Gwynedd 1910-1990

by

Roy Sloan

ISBN: 0-86381-281-3

Cover: Anne Lloyd Morris

First published in 1994 by Gwasg Carreg Gwalch,
Iard yr Orsaf, Llanrwst, Gwynedd, Wales.

☎ 0492 642031

Printed and published in Wales

Contents

Introduction and Acknowledgements

The sixteen stories which make up this book have been chosen in order to provide a broad view of the types of flying accidents which have taken place within the geographical boundaries of Gwynedd. These stories span a period of eighty years; from 1910, when Robert Loraine had the dubious distinction of being the first aviator to crash in the county, to the early 1990s, by which time literally hundreds of crashes had occurred in North Wales.

With such a vast number of accidents to choose from, it might appear that narrowing the field down to little more than a dozen examples was being selective in the extreme, and while this was partly true, with many interesting tales having to be omitted, some, on the other hand, were self selecting. No account could be regarded as complete without including the story of the Aer Lingus Dakota which plunged, out of control, into a mountain bog in Snowdonia, thus becoming the region's worst civil aviation disaster to date, or the series of high ground crashes during World War II which were to have such a profound influence upon a locally based RAF doctor in his efforts to rescue injured aircrew — efforts from which sprang the present day Mountain Rescue Organisation of the Royal Air Force, or the account of a V-bomber crew's remarkable escape from their doomed aircraft as it flew over Anglesey.

I have added to the list what I hope is a representative sample of crashes from all periods of aviation history in Gwynedd, with the objective of illustrating some of the many dangers of the air and how aircraft, while flying in this corner of Wales have fallen victim to these dangers.

Since the early years of aviation, technology has advanced in leaps and bounds, sometimes at a phenomenal rate, making flying immeasurably more sophisticated in the 1990s than in the primitive days of the pioneers, but in some respects the fundamental considerations of air safety remain unchanged. If flying is regarded as the interaction of man and machine in a hostile and unforgiving element — the air — then the problem is twofold: a) how to achieve total reliability of the machine, and b) how to eliminate all human weakness and laxity from its controller.

Neither aim can in any way be fully accomplished of course; to do so would be to reach a state of perfection impossible in this world. However advanced the technology becomes, however lengthy and thorough a pilot's training, the possibility of failure always exists. Systems and structures develop faults despite every precaution by their designers while even the most professional of pilots sometimes become careless and let their standards slip. In consequence aircraft continue to crash. Frequently, accidents result from a chain of events originating in component breakdown or human mistakes which in themselves are relatively innocuous and not fatal, but are often compounded by other circumstances, entirely unrelated to the original error, which then seem to lead inexorably to disaster. I have endeavoured to include some examples in the present volume.

The reader will discover that the book concentrates in the main on accidents to military aircraft. This is simply because of the fact that military aviation has predominated in the county. Also, there is a concentration upon accidents which have taken place in Snowdonia and again this is because the area, being mountainous and therefore naturally hazardous to aviation, has seen more than its fair share of crashes. Indeed, as the highest ground in England and Wales is to be found in Gwynedd, then it is not surprising that so many flying accidents have occurred here. Mountains and aircraft do not mix and all pilots who ignore or make light of the risks involved do so at their peril.

Since the period of World War II a great deal of wreckage has been left at crash locations in the hills, where it has lain for years without being unduly disturbed. That is until recent times, when the disappearance of many items became increasingly common, either plundered by souvenir hunters or removed by the Snowdonia National Park authorities, whose wish it was to clear all the sites. Whether this has been a wise plan on the part of the authorities is open to question as there are arguments both for and against such a policy. While some — especially aviation historians — might view wreckage as a form of memorial to the men who died in these accidents, other individuals with different perspectives and responsibilities see the crash sites as nothing more than attractions for ever-growing numbers of visitors, not all of whom would be competent hillwalkers. These visitors could easily find themselves, either through lack of skill or equipment, in perilous situations, thus adding to the chances of mishaps and misadventures, some of which would inevitably end in tragedy. Far better, according to the argument, to remove the remaining wreckage and place the more substantial items in museums, where they can be seen in comfort and safety.

To express a personal opinion, I feel that, as an aviation enthusiast who is also a keen hillwalker and climber, the interest of Snowdonia's mountains has been diminished for me by the clearance of aircraft crash sites. Pieces of wreckage put into a museum or private hands can become nothing more than a somewhat dry collection of objects, accurately identified and captioned perhaps, but uninspiring nonetheless. On the other hand, when *in situ* these relics had the capacity, especially for those with knowledge of local aviation history, to form a direct and effective link with the past, a link that seemed to fire the imagination and made that past so real. Sadly, this is no longer the case and I regret the loss.

The primary sources of information used in compiling the stories told here include RAF archives, newspaper reports, Civil Aviation Authority accident bulletins, Department of Trade crash investigation reports and publications of the now defunct Snowdonia Aviation Historical Group and Eighth Air Force Research Group Wales. Additionally, I have made use of the books listed in the bibliography.

In the course of my research I have been fortunate to receive assistance from many persons willing to share with me their experiences and knowledge. I am particularly grateful to fellow aviation enthusiasts Dafydd Roberts and Arthur Evans, both of whom have patiently garnered, over a period of many years, a wealth of detail on the Snowdonia accidents. Others I must thank are: William Jones, the late Owen Owens, Eric Hughes, the late Jack Leaversuch, Michael Bayley Hughes, Ellis Lewis, Ace Schultz, Jack Bohanna, (son of the late Mr J. Bohanna), Ernest Naish, the late Evan Jones, Hugh Williams, Richard Hughes, Idris Owen, Robert Hughes, Mrs Mair Williams, Mrs Mona Jones, Mrs A. Thomas, William Roberts and Frank Butler. I remain indebted to them all for their generous help.

Roy Sloan,
Brynsiencyn.

8

Chapter 1

A First Flight and a First Crash

Life in the Anglesey village of Llanfair-yng-Nghornwy in 1910 was no different to what it had been during the year before or the one before that. Indeed, ten years into the twentieth century, the pattern of existence in Llanfair-yng-Nghornwy was essentially unchanged from that of the nineteenth century. People lived much as they always had; their simple, pastoral lives dominated by agriculture and the traditional crafts of the countryside.

Located in the north west corner of Anglesey, near the wild, rugged coastline of Carmel Head, the village was the remotest on the island, being connected to the outside world by nothing better than a primitive track. Horse and cart transport prevailed, as it did in Anglesey generally, and while a few motor cars were to be seen on the island's roads, that other great invention of the period, the aeroplane, was in 1910 as foreign as it could possibly be to the villagers of Llanfair-yng-Nghornwy. Aviation was something entirely beyond their ken, at least until Wednesday 10 August of that year, when this state of affairs was unexpectedly and dramatically reversed.

It had been a day of hot sunshine, causing a shimmering heat haze to spread over land and sea, though by early evening the worst of the heat was over and the air had begun to cool. At 7.00 p.m. a group of children were standing outside the village chapel waiting for that evening's Band of Hope meeting to start. As they chatted noisily, in the manner of all children, they saw what looked to them like a huge bird, the largest they had ever seen, appear from the direction of the sea and glide silently down towards the village. To the youngsters' intense excitement the strange bird landed in a field some distance away. All thoughts of the Band of Hope were immediately abandoned as they ran to the field, impatient to see what this enormous creature could possibly be. When they got closer, however, they realised that it was not a bird at all, but an aeroplane, of all things! This sensational event caused the excitement to rise to fever pitch.

What the children had seen was, in fact, the first aircraft ever to fly in Gwynedd and the first to make a forced landing — its silent glide was caused by an engine which had stopped through lack of fuel. But who was the pilot of this aerial craft, a Farman Biplane to be precise, which had brought such drama to Llanfair-yng-Nghornwy? His name was Robert Loraine, a pioneer British aviator, who, during that week in August was taking part in the famous Flying Meeting held at Blackpool. While at the seaside resort, he was making clandestine preparations to attempt an aviation record and in so doing, fulfil one of his ambitions; to fly from Holyhead to Dublin and thus become the first airman to cross the Irish Sea. Having secretly planned the flight in collaboration with an old and trusted friend, George Smart, who made all the necessary arrangements at Holyhead, Loraine took the opportunity afforded by Wednesday's fine weather and departed from Blackpool early in the morning, with the intention of flying along the North Wales coast until he reached his destination.

He left at 6.30 a.m., followed shortly afterwards in a car by his mechanic, Jules Vedrines, a fierce, quarrelsome Frenchman who had his brother, Emil, with him. While both were employed to keep the Farman airworthy, Jules' skills in this respect were unrivalled but Emil's, on the other hand, were woefully inadequate. In reality he was nothing more than a sop to the aggressive Jules, who demanded that his brother joined him while he, Jules, worked in England. He hated the English and did not want to be alone in a country whose inhabitants he regarded with the deepest mistrust.

Loraine's flight did not go to plan, however. Emil had rigged the biplane's controls incorrectly and though the machine flew as it should, an excessive amount of strain was imposed not only on the control cables but also the pilot's nerves! When he saw the invitingly smooth grass of Rhos-on-Sea golf links, near Colwyn Bay, he decided not to push his luck any further and landed immediately. By the time Vedrines had caught up with him and corrected the Farman's wrongly adjusted controls, most of the day had passed and it was well after 5.00 p.m. when Loraine took off from the golf links, to the accompaniment of cheers and hoorays from a huge crowd of onlookers.

Theoretically, the task of navigating to Holyhead should have been a simple matter; following the railway line, for example, was an almost foolproof way of achieving this objective, but the biplane's pilot chose instead to fly his machine along the coast of Anglesey, past Point Lynas and Cemaes. Considering that much of this area was by then obscured by heat haze, the choice of route was, perhaps, slightly unwise in the circumstances. For one thing, the chances of inadvertently flying out to sea were increased — which is precisely what happened in this case. Loraine, never the most competent of aviators, it has to be said, became thoroughly disorientated and wandered far from the safety of the land, heading seaward for mile upon mile and getting deeper into trouble with every minute that passed. His excuse for this lapse was, believe it or not, that he fell asleep.

Eventually, through a combination of common sense and sheer luck he managed to extricate himself from a situation which could have proved fatal. With a rapidly emptying fuel tank adding a sense of urgency to his calculations he used the sun's position to work out an approximate course which he hoped would bring him back to the Anglesey coast. It did, and not a moment too soon; one mile from shore the last drops of petrol were sucked into the engine's cylinders to deliver a few more seconds of effort before the 50 h.p. Gnome spluttered and coughed to a stop.

Gliding earthwards, Loraine could see a rocky coastline ahead, beyond which there were fields, one of which would soon become his landing ground. To his relief he touched down safely and came to a halt without any damage to his machine. Within a short space of time he found himself surrounded by a crowd of wildly excited children. He did not know where he was but later he was able to ascertain that he had made his forced landing at Bryn Goelcerth Farm, Llanfair-yng-Nghornwy, only a few miles from his intended destination. Those few miles, though little more than an aerial hop, were to cost him dear, however.

On the following day, Smart, who had been at Holyhead anxiously awaiting his friend's arrival came to see Llanfair-yng-Nghornwy for himself and was not impressed: 'It was a strip of wilderness,' he said, 'that could only be reached by eight miles of execrable cart-tracks up and down impossible gradients over outcrops of rock and shale.' In this out of the way place the biplane remained for two days, grounded by strong winds which made the brief flight to Holyhead an impossibility. On Friday, 12 August, with the wind abating a little, Loraine could not contain his impatience any longer and decided to take a chance. With the help of some villagers, described rather uncharitably by the *Manchester Guardian's* reporter as 'Weird Welsh Islanders', the aircraft was rolled to the top of a slope so that a downhill run would assist the machine to gather speed quickly.

But any advantage gained was nullified because the take-off would be downwind and therefore likely to be longer than a normal into-wind run. Loraine, once more, was guilty of misjudgement. As he admitted himself: 'I could feel it [the wind] pressing and pushing down, always down.' Unable to gain more than fifteen feet of height he soon found himself struggling to clear a small hummock which obstructed his path. He failed to do so and crashed, badly damaging the Farman, though he himself escaped injury. Through his mistake, Loraine became the first pilot to suffer a flying accident in Gwynedd.

The crash left his biplane so broken that the subsequent repair was tantamount to a rebuild, a task which took the Vedrines brothers until early September to complete. As the work could not be done in the open, a temporary hangar was erected in order to provide shelter for the aircraft and also living accommodation for the French mechanics. During their stay at Llanfair-yng-Nghornwy, the brothers exhibited a fondness for drink and the company of females which scandalised the deeply religious Welsh community, whose puritanical outlook, bred by a long tradition of Calvanistic Methodism, could not have been in greater contrast to that of the pleasure seeking Frenchmen.

Meanwhile, after the accident, Loraine, who earned his living as a professional actor, left Anglesey for London, where he had acting commitments. He was, in fact, a very successful actor-manager who could count no less a person that the great playwright George Bernard Shaw among his closest friends. Indeed, the childless Shaw treated him more like a surrogate son than a friend. Loraine had been associated with the production of Shaw's plays and had, for instance, taken 'Man and Superman' to New York in the early years of the century and thereafter toured the United States, appearing in the play. A colourful, flamboyant man, Loraine possessed a complex personality, combining artistic sensibility with a love of action and adventure. He was in Paris during January

1908 and while there he saw Henry Farman fly his biplane, then in July 1909 he returned to France to witness Louis Bleriot make his historic flight across the English Channel. The sensation created by this flight and the fame it brought Bleriot had a profound effect upon Loraine. Here was an opportunity for him to satisfy his thirst for adventure and simultaneously earn the adulation of the crowds, which his actor's temperament found so gratifying. The attractions of aviation were irresistible; he decided that he was going to become a pilot.

At that time, flying was an expensive sport, available only to the wealthy — a category to which Loraine belonged without any doubt. His successful tours of the United States netted a personal fortune of £40,000 for him — a huge sum in 1910 — which he then proceeded to spend with almost reckless abandon in order to finance his flying exploits.

Back at Llanfair-yng-Nghornwy, thanks to the heroic efforts of Jules Vedrines the aircraft was ready by Sunday 4 September to take to the air once again. The mechanic, himself a frustrated aviator who lacked sufficient money to fly, fussed over last minute adjustments while Loraine climbed into the pilot's seat, watched as usual, by a large and enthusiastic crowd.

With a light wind blowing and favourable weather conditions it looked as if success might at last be within reach but the flight was, in fact, doomed before it began. Unfortunately, the field chosen for the take-off was reclaimed bog which had retained much of its marshy character. The engine was started and away went the Farman, only to come to a halt after travelling just a few yards as its wheels began to sink into the soft ground. With a sharp crack the undercarriage and centre section collapsed, pinning Loraine by his legs. Onlookers quickly freed him from the wreckage and a doctor, who happened to be in the crowd, examined him and found that he was suffering from nothing worse than badly bruised limbs. As his biographer aptly remarked: 'Strange that no one had ever noticed there was bog beneath that ground.'

After this latest setback so disheartened was Loraine that he came close to abandoning his attempt on the Holyhead-Dublin crossing but his friend, Smart, persuaded him to make one further effort. The mangled biplane — little more than a heap of splintered wood and torn fabric — was then loaded on to a humble farm-cart and taken, ignominiously, by road to Holyhead, there to be repaired for the second time by the long-suffering though faithful Vedrines, who worked at a pace which can only be described as frantic, in order to complete the task within a week.

But why such a desperate hurry? Two considerations were responsible for the haste: first, Loraine's fear, groundless as it turned out, that a rival might be planning a similar flight, and secondly, the pilot's acting commitments in London, which allowed him only one more free weekend in Anglesey.

On Sunday 11 September he finally became airborne and was able to embark upon a record breaking flight which he had dearly wanted to attempt. It was a remarkable and exciting flight whose details are beyond the scope of the present volume, but suffice it to say that Loraine almost reached the Irish coast, coming down in the sea a mere two hundred yards from the shore. After all the trials and tribulations of the past few weeks this was a bitter disappointment to him and his team, to say the least.

Because he had failed to reach land, even though it was only by a hairsbreadth, he could not claim to have completed the crossing but nevertheless his was a fine performance. The Royal Aero Club presented him with a silver medal and his friends from the theatrical world gave him a silver statuette representing the marriage of Art and Aviation embodied in his person.

Robert Loraine achieved little of note in aviation subsequently but Jules Vedrines, the quick tempered and anglophobic Frenchman went on to become one of his country's leading aviators, winning prizes and honours galore. In 1912, for instance, he set up a world speed record of 108 m.p.h. and won the Gordon Bennett cup. He survived the First World War but was killed in a flying accident in April 1919, by which time he was a hugely popular figure in France.

As for Llanfair-yng-Nghornwy, once the momentous events of that August in 1910 were over, life in the village returned to its usual slack pace. With Loraine, his Farman biplane and the two French mechanics gone forever, all that remained, besides a few pieces of wood and doped linen kept as souvenirs of the crashes, was a marvellous tale told and re-told on many a hearth over the years and which became part of folk memory in this quiet corner of Anglesey.

Chapter 2

A Trio of 1930s Accidents

Today there are scores of private pilots active in Gwynedd. They come from a wide variety of backgrounds and whatever their status, they have one thing in common — a love of flying, and the resources necessary to pursue this exciting and adventurous activity. Even those with quite modest means can fly if they want to, though this has not always been the case. Back in the 1930s the situation was very different; only the wealthy could afford to own and operate a private aircraft, if they had the inclination to do so. In Gwynedd the number of individuals so disposed was small, indeed they could be counted on the fingers of one hand.

Prominent among this exclusive group was W. Prys Evans of Broom Hall, Pwllheli. The son of a rich landowner, Colonel O.J. Lloyd Evans, he had, upon the death of his father, inherited Broom Hall and its associated estate. Evans took a keen interest in aviation and in 1932, at the age of 27, he obtained his private pilot's licence — one of the first in the region to do so. A year previously he had unsuccessfully contested the Parliamentary seat of Caernarfonshire as a National Government candidate but received the highest number of votes ever given to a Tory in the county. His other credentials included presidency of the Pwllheli Conservative Club, British Legion and Pwllheli Gliding Club. He was also a magistrate and director of two local newspapers, the *North Wales Chronicle* and *North Wales Pioneer*.

After gaining his licence, Evans purchased his own aircraft, building a hangar for it, and an airstrip at Broom Hall, from which he flew regularly, making local flights as well as venturing further afield to Scotland and Ireland, for instance. However, it all came to an end in April 1937 when his de Havilland Puss Moth (G-AAXW) crashed on take-off, killing its young pilot.

On Tuesday 6 April Evans was preparing for a flight to his brother's home in Surrey, where he intended to stay for a week. Shortly before 1.00 p.m. his chauffeur, Thomas Owen, filled the Puss Moth's tank with twenty gallons of fuel and placed his employer's suitcase in the cabin. The engine was then started, without any difficulty, and while it was warming up in the hangar, Evans walked out into the middle of the field to test the wind's direction and strength by holding his handkerchief aloft. This somewhat crude method was explained by the fact that the windsock had been taken down for the winter, a period when little flying took place at Broom Hall. The handkerchief's limpness indicated only the lightest movement of air.

After warming up, the aircraft was taxied to the far corner of the airstrip and the take-off run started. To Thomas Owen, who watched the machine gather speed while he was closing the hangar doors, everything appeared to be normal. He had seen Evans take off many times previously and this occasion seemed to be no different. Expecting the Puss Moth to become airborne at any moment, he briefly turned his back on the scene in order to concentrate on the job of securing the hangar door, but when he turned around again the aircraft was still on the ground.

Though no pilot, Owen knew the machine should have been in the air by then. With mounting apprehension he watched as G-AAXW ran the whole length of the airstrip before disappearing from the chauffeur's line of vision. Suddenly it came back into view, rising sharply before diving with a terrific crash into a ploughed field beyond the airstrip.

Working in this field was a rabbit catcher, Thomas Ellis, from the nearby village of Chwilog. Standing by the field's boundary wall he saw the Puss Moth coming directly towards him. Instinctively, he ducked and watched in horror as the aircraft, barely airborne, collided with the top of the wall and then reared up almost alongside him, before nose diving into the field. Momentum carried the machine for many yards before it finally came to a halt, facing the way it had come. There was no post-crash fire and so it was relatively easy for Ellis, who reached the aircraft almost as soon as it had stopped moving, to make an attempt at rescue, but his effort was in vain. Tearing open the cabin door, he found Evans had been fatally injured and was on the point of death. Dragging the moribund pilot out of the wreckage, Ellis did his best to ease the man's final moments. The situation was not without some irony; one of the region's richest landowners comforted, as his life ebbed away, by a humble rabbit catcher, a poor man, yet one whose humanity when faced with a fellow human being's

16

death, counted for so much more than material wealth. Then the chauffeur arrived, breathless and greatly agitated, but there was nothing for him to do except help in the sad task of removing his late master's body from the crash site.

At the subsequent inquest, both lay and expert testimony could not satisfactorily explain why the aircraft had failed to become airborne. Though an Air Ministry investigator, Major S.J. Fill, had closely examined the wreckage he was unable to pinpoint a cause for the accident. The engine was functioning normally and the Puss Moth was not overloaded — in fact it was 200 lbs below the weight limit. Thomas Owen revealed that a week before the crash Evans suspected that water had contaminated the Moth's fuel. 'We drained the petrol,' he stated, 'but found no water and after a trial flight Mr Evans reported everything to be satisfactory.'

If there was no technical failure, could the crash have been caused by taking off downwind? This means, invariably, a longer than usual ground run and is only undertaken as a last resort or in an emergency. But in the case of the Puss Moth, the evidence was inconclusive. When asked by the coroner if he had noticed the wind direction on the day of the accident, Thomas Owen said he had not, while Thomas Ellis, when the question was put to him could only reply that it was his 'impression the aircraft was travelling approximately down wind.' The lack of certainty served only to weaken his statement. It is possible, of course, that the wind was light enough — as indicated by the limp handkerchief — for conditions to be regarded as calm, and therefore take-off could be in almost any direction. A further possibility is that Evans, without the benefit of a proper windsock had misjudged the wind's speed and direction.

Thomas Ellis then went on to describe to the coroner and inquest jury what happened after he saw the aircraft approaching; 'When it was forty yards from me,' he said, 'it was still on the ground. When twenty yards away it rose a little, came straight for me, and I ducked behind the wall. As it passed over, there was a noise and I saw the wheels strike the top of the wall. The aeroplane appeared to rise to the height of the tree tops and then it crashed nose first into the ploughed field about one hundred yards from where I stood.'

To judge from this description it seems that Evans, as the wall drew ever closer, must have pulled the stick right back in a desperate attempt to gain height but in doing so he forced the Puss Moth into such a nose-up attitude that after clipping the wall, the aircraft stalled and dived into the ground. Whatever actually took place during that abortive take-off, whether it was pilot error or some other factor which brought about failure, the accident was a tragic event which precipitated the death of a young man.

During the early 1930s Evans and the few other civilian pilots in Gwynedd had the skies to themselves, but in 1935 plans were afoot in faraway London which would change the situation and bring military aviation, for the first time, to the region. These plans, drawn up by the Air Ministry as part of the Government's rearmament schemes, called for the establishment of a permanent RAF bombing and air gunnery training base near the town of Pwllheli. Once this became known, however, the project stirred up a hornet's nest of local opposition, principally from the Welsh Nationalists, who marshalled all their forces into a determined campaign to foil the Air Ministry. But despite every objection, and in the face of the most vociferous protestations the construction of RAF Penrhos, as it was to be known, went ahead. The result was the famous arson attack upon the half completed airfield by the Nationalists in September 1936.

Early in February 1937 Penrhos opened as No. 5 Armament Training Camp and from then onwards the sight of military aircraft in the quiet skies of Llŷn became commonplace. Groups of aircraft, usually from Flying Training Schools came to Penrhos for periods of four or five weeks so that crews could learn the techniques of bombing and air gunnery. Often these machines would arrive and depart *en masse*, providing an impressive spectacle for onlookers but sometimes things went badly wrong, as they did on 29 November 1937, for instance, when no less than three aircraft crashed.

On that day a squadron of eighteen Hawker Hart Trainers and Audaxes, belonging to No. 2 Flying Training School at RAF Brize Norton, in Oxfordshire, had set off on a cross country flight to Penrhos. Their route took them first to RAF Sealand, near Chester, from where the squadron would then follow the North Wales coast to their destination. Originally, twenty machines were due to leave Brize Norton but after eighteen had become airborne a telephone message from Penrhos warned that local weather conditions were deteriorating and that thick fog and heavy rain was likely to be encountered by the aircraft upon arrival.

After landing at Sealand, ten pilots decided not to pursue their journey, wisely preferring to remain on the ground. There is a lot of truth in the old saying that it is better to be on the ground wishing you were in the air than in the air wishing you were on the ground. One pilot returned to base while seven of his colleagues elected to continue with their flight. No difficulties arose until the aircraft reached Caernarfon, where a lowering cloudbase of 2,000 feet was encountered, forcing the flight to descend in order to maintain visual contact with the ground. Fifteen miles on, the seven machines ran into a rainstorm which pushed them down to 600 feet, at which unsafe height the visibility was little more than two miles. Having followed the coast past Aberdaron and Bardsey Island in similarly adverse weather, they turned eastwards, heading for Abersoch and finally Pwllheli, arriving at 12.30 p.m. Leading three of the aircraft, Hawker Hart K5837 and Audaxes K7392 and K7479, was Flight Sergeant Charles Ridd, who, after observing the beach at Pwllheli, signalled a turn towards Penrhos, now only two miles away, but as he flew towards his destination, contact with the other machines was unfortunately lost because of the low cloud. Almost within sight of their goal, luck had run out for the group. Once the trio of aircraft became leaderless, they were unable to locate the airfield and all were forced to make emergency landings at various locations.

Closest to Penrhos was Audax K7479 which, according to the *North Wales Chronicle*, emerged from the fog at a very low altitude, heading for the Town Hall clock tower at Pwllheli. Continuing its account, the *Chronicle* added: 'The pilot had to open the throttle quickly to avoid hitting the tower and with great skill he avoided coming in contact with the Tabernacle Baptist Chapel tower. The machine headed in the direction of the airfield, skimming over the tree tops of Lleyn Street.' After this rather frightening roof level flight the pilot, it seems, had had enough and came down in a field near the village of Efailnewydd, barely two miles from Penrhos. The Audax suffered severe damage though its two occupants were unhurt, and no doubt thankful to be back on the ground.

Unhappily, the second Audax did not fare so well. It flew for another three miles before narrowly missing a farmhouse at

Fourcrosses, whereupon the 22 year old pilot attempted to land in an all too small field and was unable to stop his aircraft before it crashed, with fatal force, into a wall. The impact killed him and seriously injured his passenger.

Meanwhile, the Hart remained airborne, flying in a northerly direction, which meant that every passing second took it further away from Penrhos. Blundering along in the murk, the Hart's pilot continued for a further twelve miles before encountering cloud obscured rising ground at Nebo, close to the village of Penygroes. Because he was sandwiched between dense fog above and the earth below (and a thoroughly unpalatable sandwich it made) the pilot had very limited room for manoeuvre. Unable to deal with the unexpected hazard, he stalled his aircraft, which then crash landed in a marshy field and slid for fifty yards, leaving a trail of wreckage before colliding with, and demolishing part of a stone wall. Suffering from head injuries, both pilot and passenger were quickly rescued by farm workers and taken to hospital at Bangor.

Immediately after these events, as was usual following serious accidents, an RAF Board of Inquiry was set up to investigate the circumstances which had led to the crashes, but more unusually, a question was also asked in the House of Commons, where the Opposition wanted to know how the RAF had lost three aircraft in one day.

As recorded in *Hansard* for 1 December, Mr McEntee, Member for Walthamstow, requested an explanatory statement from the Under Secretary of State for Air and after being given a brief outline of the facts in reply, the MP went on to ask if a public inquiry would be held. The answer was in the negative because, it was felt, the RAF's own investigation would be sufficient to elicit all the necessary details.

When that inquiry eventually completed its task and the time came to apportion blame, the Board's members expressed some criticism of the inadequate weather forecasting facilities at Penrhos, where, it was recommended that a qualified meteorologist should be employed. It took more than a year for this deficiency to be remedied, when, in February 1939 a meteorological office was finally opened.

As mentioned previously, aircraft which arrived in large groups also tended to leave Penrhos in likewise manner, and while the vast majority of flights reached their home base safely, some did not. One such departure, which ended in the death of three airmen, took place on 17 September 1937. Like many other local crashes, before and after this particular example, much of the fault lay in that fatal combination of high ground and low cloud, so frequently found in North Wales, with its mountains and associated bad weather.

During September No. 220 Squadron, Coastal Command, from RAF Bircham Newton, Norfolk, had been training at the Llŷn airfield. On the 17th their stay came to an end and in the course of the morning fourteen of the squadron's Avro Ansons were being prepared for the flight back to East Anglia. All the aircraft got safely into the air later that morning and set off, in moderately good weather, on the first leg of their journey — a coast hugging flight to RAF Sealand, where the squadron would land. Soon after becoming airborne, however, one of the Ansons developed engine trouble and had to return to Penrhos, where, after landing, it collided with a stationary aircraft, causing damage to both machines and injuring one man. It was a bad start, especially to those of a superstitious nature, because the flight was now reduced in number to the proverbially unlucky thirteen. The aircraft continued along the coast until, shortly before noon, they were approaching the headland of Penmaenmawr, where a blanket of low cloud and mist obscured this prominent feature and also the smaller headland of Penmaenbach beyond. Both rose steeply from the sea, the former to a height of 1,000 feet and the latter to 800 feet.

The squadron's leader signalled visually to the others that they were to climb but when they emerged into clearer air there were only twelve aircraft. Sadly, the missing Anson, K6227, had met a calamitous end; it had crashed into the sea and the three crew members were dead.

It seems that the pilot, 24 year old Sergeant William Rimmer, did not see his leader's hand signal (apparently RT communication, which most certainly would have prevented the accident, was not available at that time) and while everyone else promptly disappeared into cloud he was left on his own, flying at a low altitude — 300 feet or lower according to some witnesses. He missed Penmaenmawr headland, though whether it was by chance or not we shall never know, and then headed for the Conwy estuary, unaware that some three miles ahead lay the 800 foot high bulk of Penmaenbach.

If we assume that Sergeant Rimmer followed the advice given in Pilot's Notes for flying an Anson in bad visibility — reducing airspeed to a sedate 85 mph and lowering flaps 20° — then he would have less than two minutes before hitting the obstruction. Though the aircraft's speed cannot now be ascertained with any degree of accuracy, we can be sure that it was low enough not only for the pilot to see the rising ground ahead but also to have time to react — a luxury not usually afforded to pilots unlucky enough to be in such a perilous situation.

Rimmer, probably in a tense, alert state, must have become aware of a sudden darkening in the greyish white vapours which alerted him to danger. Out of the gloom a soft nebulous shape was revealed, which rapidly resolved itself into the tangible form of solid rock and earth that was Penmaenbach headland. Instantly Rimmer pulled the stick back and applied left rudder, putting the Anson into a steep climbing turn to port. By his quick action he managed to avoid crashing headlong into the ground, but in averting one disaster he created another, which he and his crew failed to survive. Engine power had not been increased in the emergency and in its steep climb the aircraft lost flying speed and stalled. There was insufficient height to recover, as a result of which the doomed machine plunged nose first into the sea, a few hundred yards from shore.

The accident was watched by a gang of platelayers working on the nearby railway line, which runs through Penmaenbach by means of a tunnel. One man telephoned the police from a lineside cabin while his workmates ran to the beach to see if they could help, but the Anson had disappeared from view and there was no sign of its occupants. The local police, meanwhile, had organised a rescue party with the help of fishermen from Conwy, who used their boats to reach the crashed aircraft, which by then was exposed by the ebbing tide. Inside the tangled wreckage they found the bodies of the pilot and his two colleagues, Aircraftsmen Michael Kervin and Kenneth Butcher.

But what had become of the other twelve Ansons? After losing Rimmer they had flown for only a short distance before another pilot became disorientated in the murky conditions and found himself separated from the flight. Now on his own and unsure of his position, he came upon the Conwy estuary and turned south to follow the river, probably under the impression, initially at least, that he was flying along the coast. Whether or not he knew that he was in a valley, the pilot was jeopardising the safety of his aircraft by maintaining this course. To fly in reduced visibility along a valley bounded by high ground is to run the risk of being trapped in a dead-end, which is often a description that not only befits the valley's topography but also that of the unfortunate pilot's fate.

Luckily, this particular pilot must have realised that he was in the Conwy Valley and escaped by making a 180° turn while he still had room to do so. Returning the way he had come, he flew past the town of Conwy and out to sea, passing low over some fishing boats, completely unaware that the vessels had been commandeered by the police to search for the crashed Anson from his own squadron.

For their part, those on the water assumed, naturally enough, the approaching aircraft was engaged on the same mission as themselves and so they were mystified to see the machine disappear quickly eastwards. The pilot, having regained his bearings, and with no inkling of the drama below, had set a course for Sealand, arriving there shortly after his eleven colleagues. It was only then that he learnt of the accident. Later that day, what remained of Anson K6227 was dragged to the shore by RAF personnel, assisted by civilian volunteers.

At the inquest into the deaths of Rimmer, Butcher and Kervin, the jury, in passing their verdict added a perceptive rider, 'It is hoped,' their foreman said, 'that in areas like this, every possible attention is paid to weather reports. We, like many other people, are alarmed at the increase in RAF tragedies in recent months . . .' [1937, in comparison to 1936, saw an increase of almost 50% in the number of aircrew killed in flying accidents.] 'We feel,' added the foreman, 'that a reference of this sort will bring all pilots to realise the conditions existing in areas like this.' Superstition or not, it had been a case of unlucky thirteen for No. 220 Squadron that day in September 1937.

Chapter 3

Mountain Rescue is Born

One aspect of aviation in Gwynedd during the Second World War was a huge rise in the number of flying accidents, particularly in the mountains of Snowdonia, where aircraft came to grief with a frequency quite unknown before 1940. Intensive flying training activity, bad weather, low cloud blanketing the hills, inexperienced aircrew operating in unsuitable conditions or at night, and navigational errors were among the most common causes of accidents. With every aircraft that was destroyed and its crew killed on some desolate, cloud-hidden mountainside, there was, besides the material loss, a much greater human loss, not only in terms of valuable aircrew for the RAF but also for the families of the crash victims. If an efficient, well equipped and well trained rescue organisation had been set up at the outset then perhaps many more lives would have been saved, but few in the RAF, at that time, foresaw how the situation in Snowdonia and other parts of upland Britain would develop.

At the beginning of the War, rescue parties using civilian volunteers and personnel from local RAF and Army camps were put together on an *ad hoc* basis, with little equipment and even less training. The police took a leading part in organising some of these rescue parties, as they did, for example, in the case of a Blackburn Skua which crashed into Elidir Fawr mountain during a raging snowstorm in February 1941.

Shortly before noon on the 19th, Sergeant Jones, on duty at Llanberis police station, was informed that an aircraft accident had taken place on Elidir Fawr, a 3,000 feet high peak two miles to the east of the town. The bearer of this news was a local hillfarmer, William Jones of Fron Farm, Nant Peris, who, an hour previously had been on the mountainside tending his sheep in the blizzard. Whilst shepherding his flock to ensure their survival in the adverse conditions, he heard the noise of an aircraft flying overhead, in the direction of Elidir Fawr. The farmer listened for a few seconds, before the steady beat of the aircraft's engine was abruptly ended by the sounds of a crash. Moments after the impact a break

24

appeared in the clouds and visibility was good enough for William Jones to see debris being blown everywhere. He also caught a glimpse of wreckage on fire before the clouds closed in once again, and as he hurried downwards to raise the alarm, his ears were ringing with the sharp sounds of ammunition exploding in the fire's heat.

On being told of the crash, the police sergeant at Llanberis immediately got together a search party made up of local civilians, who were soon trudging upwards through the snow. Progress was not rapid, impeded as it was by visibility of no more than a few yards and ground made treacherous by the icy conditions. However, after three hours of toilsome effort the summit of Elidir Fawr was finally attained, where the party split into smaller groups to carry out a localised search. It did not take long for two members of the party, Hugh Hughes, the Nant Peris schoolmaster and Alun Jones, a farm worker, to spot the wreckage amongst boulders only two hundred feet below the mountain top. Had the Skua's pilot chosen to fly at a marginally higher altitude he might well have escaped the fate that befell him.

Because of the atrocious weather and rocky ground the men of the rescue party were not able to reach the wreckage, only getting close enough to see a Royal Navy coat with officers gold braid on it, lying in the debris. In the absence of any sign of life it was assumed that the pilot and any crew (at this stage it was not known how many occupants the aircraft had) were dead and removal of the body, or bodies, would be left until the following day. Sergeant Jones was adamant that this task should be completed within twenty four hours as it would be improper to leave the corpses on the hillside for any length of time, especially when there were many foxes known to be in the vicinity, he said, and there would be no telling the damage they might cause if given the chance.

At 10.30 a.m. on the 20th the police sergeant was preparing to climb Elidir Fawr once again, but now his party was made up of military men — a group of soldiers, and two armourers from RAF Penrhos. They arrived at the crash site at 1.00 p.m. On the mountain, conditions were still bad, with a thick covering of loose, powdery snow to contend with. In places it had formed into drifts five feet high, causing the searchers great difficulty in their unpleasant job of looking for bodies. Eventually they discovered the remains of two men, both badly mutilated and burnt. Meanwhile, the armourers collected every round of ammunition they could find and removed a Lewis gun from the ashes of the rear cockpit. The aircraft also carried four Browning machine-guns in its wings but so badly were they damaged that they were left behind as scrap, to be recovered later by the MU salvage party. Subsequently, the Skua (serial number L3054) and its two man crew — a 20 year old pilot and 26 year old observer — were identified as belonging to No. 801 Squadron of the Fleet Air Arm based at St Merryn, in Cornwall.

This type of rescue effort, essentially amateurish though fully committed to the job in hand, was maintained throughout 1941 as the crashes continued unabated but in 1942 an event occurred which would bring huge and fundamental changes to the business of rescuing aircrew from accidents in the mountains; the arrival at RAF Llandwrog of Flight Lieutenant George Graham as the station's Medical Officer. A doctor with an interest in climbing, he quickly realised how inadequately searches for crashed aircraft were carried out in the nearby hills. Determined to improve matters by creating a more formal organisation, he set up a search and rescue party at Llandwrog composed of medical orderlies from the Station Sick Quarters backed up by volunteer airmen. Whenever an aircraft came down in the mountains of Snowdonia — something which happened frequently — the team would set out, in all weathers, to search for any survivors. It was, in fact, the beginning of the RAF's present day Mountain Rescue organisation.

The pioneers were, however, seriously hampered in their efforts by lack of special equipment and inexperience of mountain terrain. Their objective was to bring injured airmen as quickly and efficiently as possible from remote locations down to lower ground, for which purpose items such as stretchers and radios were essential, plus expertise in mountaincraft. In other words, adopting a more professional approach to the problem was the only way to save more lives. But despite their lack of skill and equipment, Graham and his colleagues had, by the end of 1942, brought twelve aircrew to safety and recovered thirty five bodies from eleven crashes in Snowdonia.

Two of these accidents had taken place on one day — 20

November — highlighting the frustration felt by Flight Lieutenant Graham about the inadequacies of his nascent rescue organisation. At midday Hawker Henley L3334 took off from RAF Penrhos and shortly afterwards entered low cloud in the Cwm Silyn area but unfortunately the 26 year old pilot became disorientated with the result that he flew into cliffs above Cwm Silyn and was killed instantly. Two hours later, another of Penrhos' aircraft, Anson N4981, with five crew members on board, became airborne in order to carry out a navigation exercise. Soon this machine encountered the same bank of cloud as the Henley, and into which the Anson likewise flew, never to emerge. Once in cloud, the trap was sprung and the hapless pilot, in similar fashion to his newly-deceased fellow aviator, began to follow an increasingly erratic course.

By then Graham's search party had left Llandwrog and were on their way to Cwm Silyn, where, despite the thick mist which hung over the area, they hoped to locate the crashed Henley. The search failed, however, because visibility was down to no more than a few yards, making the task of finding the aircraft in such conditions virtually impossible. It was like looking for the proverbial needle in a haystack with the added handicap of being blindfolded. Even if the wreckage had been found and the pilot had survived, by some miracle, the rescue team could have done little to help him because the Henley had impacted on cliffs inaccessible without climbing skills, which the Llandwrog team did not possess at that time.

Meanwhile, some five miles to the north, Anson N4981 was in serious trouble. It was seen flying over Nant-y-Betws at 2.30 p.m. and a few seconds later crashed into the cloud-obscured southern side of Moel Eilio. People in the valley below heard the noise of the crash and began to search the hillside for wreckage, which they found within an hour. Four of the crew were dead but one man was still alive, though injured. Sadly he died a few hours later from the effects of exposure and shock, before proper medical assistance could be got to him. The person who might have been able to save this man's life — Flight Lieutenant Graham — was leading the fruitless search in Cwm Silyn. Human error was deemed to be the cause of the Anson's crash, in that its pilot had contravened orders, and not for the first time apparently, by maintaining a dangerously low altitude considering the ground over which he was flying. On the following day, the Henley's wreckage was discovered but recovering the pilot's body proved extremely difficult — so difficult, in fact, as to be beyond the capabilities of Graham's men and the assistance of quarrymen from the nearby Nantlle Slate Quarry was sought. Experienced in the use of ropes, they were able to negotiate the steep rock face of the cliff and reach a gully where the dead man lay.

Two months after these events, on 14 January 1943 one of Llandwrog's Ansons, EG110, failed to return from a cross-country night flight. The aircraft had crashed at 8.45 p.m. on the north east slopes of Foel Grach, in the heart of the Carneddau range of mountains. On the following day, with a cloud base of 2,000 feet, a limited air search revealed nothing but at 2.00 p.m. the Anson's pilot, Pilot Officer Kenneth Archer, a 31 year old New Zealander, stumbled into a farmhouse near Talybont in the Conwy Valley. He was exhausted and in a confused state of mind. At 4.30 p.m. Graham, in company with two others from his team arrived at the farmhouse, where they found Archer still confused and incapable of providing any useful information. Having left the crash site to seek help for three injured crew members, he had no idea in which direction the aircraft lay and all he could remember was climbing a ridge and passing two lakes.

From this slender clue Graham speculated, correctly as it turned out, that the lakes could well be Llyn Dulyn and Melynllyn, and therefore the crashed Anson was to be found somewhere above, either on Foel Fras or Foel Grach. He and his two assistants proceeded to search the slopes of these mountains far into the night, only abandoning their task when a snowstorm made it impossible to continue. It was 2.00 a.m. when the three were forced to withdraw but at dawn they were out again, this time with a large party of some thirty men from Llandwrog, plus a few civilians to assist in what was to be a major search. Two groups were formed; one to go over, in a more thorough manner, the ground already covered by Graham, while he himself led the second group to a new search area. Soon, with daylight making their job so much easier, the first party found the Anson, in a gully above Llyn Dulyn. One man was still alive though suffering from a broken arm and jaw but his two friends were dead; their injuries and prolonged exposure to the bitter cold of a snowy January night had sapped their will to live. As Flight Lieutenant Graham was in the second party, contact had to be made with this party before the injured survivor could receive expert medical attention, but communication between the two groups was so poor that another ninety minutes passed before Graham was able to reach the wounded airman. Even then, the man's troubles were not over as it took three long, irksome hours for his rescuers, using an unsuitable stretcher, to get him to an ambulance.

The unsatisfactory outcome of this incident, coming so soon after the Moel Eilio crash troubled Llandwrog's Medical Officer deeply. In both cases aircrew had died primarily because the search and rescue organisation was not as efficient as it could be. Continuing lack of rescources and inadequate training was costing too many lives, he thought. The only way to improve matters permanently, in his view, was to set up an official Mountain Rescue unit, with funding from the Air Ministry in order to purchase proper equipment, rough ground vehicles, and train team members in mountaincraft. He submitted his proposals through the usual channels and after the higher echelons of the RAF and Air Ministry had been convinced by his arguments, Graham and his team found themselves provided with ropes, boots, maps, clothing, radio sets and transport. Equally important was the teaching of climbing skills to the team members, turning them into competent mountaineers, able to negotiate any kind of terrain in all weathers with confidence and safety.

Further official approval of Flight Lieutenant Graham's activities was marked by the award of a thoroughly deserved honour, the MBE, in January 1943 for his contribution to the development of mountain rescue techniques.

Six months later, on 6 July, the Llandwrog team, proud to be recognised as the first RAF Mountain Rescue Unit, opened an official log and on the same day attended their first call-out, to a Lancaster which had crashed on a hill near Llangernyw in Denbighshire. By the end of 1943 thirty three survivors had been rescued from twenty two crashes — positive proof of the team's value. Furthermore, similar units were also set up at RAF Millom in the Lake District and RAF Wigtown in south west Scotland. By the end of 1944 the number of teams in the UK had been increased to eight. Thus, from the seeds sown at one of Gwynedd's wartime airfields has grown the RAF's present day Mountain Rescue organisation, with its highly trained personnel, all volunteers, and with a range of sophisticated equipment at their disposal.

In January 1944 Flight Lieutenant Graham was sent on an overseas tour of duty. Behind him he left a team at Llandwrog which was vastly superior, in terms of manpower and resources, to the one he had begun to develop so assiduously in 1942. His unremitting and ultimately successful efforts to increase the survival chances of crashed aircrew in the mountains represented an achievement of which Graham could feel justifiably proud. Strangely however, after relinquishing his RAF commission in 1947 he had no further contact with the Mountain Rescue service which he had played such a large part in shaping. Graham died in 1980, in total obscurity.

Chapter 4

The Loss of Beaufighter X8190

One of the most popular beaches in Anglesey is to be found at Llanddwyn, near the village of Newborough, in the south western corner of the island. Every summer thousands of holidaymakers flock to the area in search of sand, sea and sunshine; ingredients which together with fine views of the mountains, make this particular beach so attractive. To reach Llanddwyn a narrow road winds for two miles through the Forestry Commission plantations of pinetrees which cover most of Newborough Warren. Not far from the start of this road a rough track can be seen leading away to the left and while a padlocked gate prevents motorists from using the track, on foot it can be a pleasant and relaxing walk which leads eventually to the beach. Until May 1992 anyone using this route would have come upon the ruins of a small, low hut-like structure built partly below ground level. After that date, however, the building was sealed and obscured from view by large quantities of sand placed upon it by the Forestry Commission. So what was the purpose of this rather strange looking hut?

Persons old enough to remember the Second World War might well have recognised it as an Anderson air-raid shelter, for that is what it was, though in this case slightly enlarged and modified. But few could guess as to why it was built in the middle of the then bare sand dunes of Newborough Warren, well away from any habitation. It was, in fact, part of a dummy airfield lighting system operated during the War as a decoy to lure any marauding German aircraft away from RAF Valley, which by the autumn of 1941 had become sufficiently important to warrant protection of this nature.

Thus Air Ministry officials expert in camouflage and deception techniques visited Anglesey to look for suitable sites close — but not too close — to Valley. They chose Newborough Warren, with its extensive coastal sand dunes, some nine miles south of the real airfield. Here, in November 1941 work began on the construction of a decoy site consisting of the standard Drem type of runway lighting pattern with the Anderson shelter from which to operate the system. On top of this shelter a small searchlight was installed, with electrical power for it and all the other lights provided by two generators. The site was intended for night use only, the lights being fixed on poles set among the sand dunes. Such decoys were known as 'Q' sites by the Air Ministry, while those intended for daytime use were designated 'K' sites (though none were built in Gwynedd).

An NCO and three airmen — Corporal Barfield, LACs Jack Leaversuch, Thomas Baldwin and Leonard Morris — operated the Newborough decoy. Each man worked a rota of three nights on duty followed by one night off, but the work was not arduous or stimulating in any way. On the contrary, the men's labours were monotonously routine: switching and testing of lights, cleaning windblown sand from lamps and generator maintenance. Control of the site was from Valley, which requested the lights to be switched on or off as necessary.

All four of the operating crew were billeted in the nearby village, where they made many friends. Indeed, one man, Jack Leaversuch, married a local girl. After the war he and his bride left Anglesey but many years later, when in retirement, the couple returned to Newborough.

Though the 'Q' type of decoy was an excellent piece of deception, it possessed one fundamental disadvantage; it could deceive both friend and foe alike with equal facility. An RAF aircraft, for example, which found itself in distress and in need of somewhere to land could easily mistake the lights for those of a genuine airfield, with fatal results! To minimise this danger the lighting pattern had two safeguards: first, a screened red bar of lights across the dummy runway threshold, visible only from an angle of 30° or less to the runway axis and second, omission of the 'T' used normally to indicate where landing should take place. Any pilot noting these departures from the usual pattern should, therefore, be aware that he was at a 'Q' site. Furthermore, the lights could also be switched off completely by the site crew if an aircraft persisted in landing.

However, it is not difficult to see that stress arising from an emergency, when the overriding concern of a pilot would be to land without delay, could cause him to overlook these safeguards. This was to be demonstrated in a tragic manner at Newborough in October 1942.

During this period the resident night fighter unit at Valley was 456 (RAAF) Squadron, operating Mk. VI Beaufighters. The unit had been formed at the airfield in June 1941 from Australian aircrew. Since August 1942 part of the squadron's duties had been to take part in what were known as 'Bullseye' exercises — exercises designed, through the co-operation of night fighter aircraft and others on the ground, such as searchlight units, to provide realistic conditions for bomber crews undergoing training.

On the night of 8 October 1942 456 Squadron was participating in a 'Bullseye', for which purpose the 'Q' site at Newborough was lit. Flying over Anglesey was Beaufighter X8190, piloted by a 20 year old Australian, Sergeant R. Scott, with his fellow countryman, 21 year old Sergeant C. Wood as the Observer/Radio Operator. Extensive layers of cloud ranging from 2,000 feet to 6,000 feet covered the island that night. Everything had been normal in the aircraft until shortly before 11.00 p.m. when the starboard engine began to lose power and soon thereafter failed completely. Scott then reported to Valley that an emergency had arisen and that he was returning to base immediately. To assist in what was clearly going to be a difficult landing he requested that the floodlight — a powerful light used to illuminate the runway threshold — be turned on. His request was complied with at once.

Following a descent from 9,000 feet through cloud the Beaufighter eventually emerged into clear air, but by the greatest misfortune it did so over Newborough where, of course, the dummy runway lamps were burning brightly, sending out their false message into the darkness. Scott saw these lights and made a fatal mistake; he assumed that he was at Valley. To his stressed mind, runway lights must have been the most welcome sight in the world at that moment, because they held out the promise of safety. So eager was he to land and so enticing was the siren-like pull of the glowing beacons below that he succumbed without hesitation and was lured down towards the trap that lay beneath X8190's wings. It is apparent that anxiety brought on by the prospect of making a single engined landing at night, coupled with a strong desire to get back on to the ground, caused Scott's lapse of vigilance. Sadly, it was an error which cost him and his companion their lives.

Drawn like a moth towards a flame, the Beaufighter rapidly lost height and headed for the 'runway' — and disaster. The aircraft's pilot noticed there was no floodlight as he had requested and once more asked for it to be switched on. Flying control at Valley timed this message at 11.03 p.m. In the operations room was Fred Stevens, one of the pilot's friends in 456 Squadron. He recollects that evening: 'I was visiting the Operations Room on the night of the accident. He (Scotty) reported returning on one engine but as he was close to base there didn't seem to be any cause for alarm. He reported sighting the runway and asked for the floodlight to be switched on. Several seconds later he again called out urgently 'Floodlight'! The controller reported it was already on but there was no reply.' At this stage the Valley controller had no idea why there had been loss of contact. He thought the aircraft was approaching the airfield and could not understand why Scott, after reporting that he had the runway in view, was unable to see the floodlight while the pilot, for his part, failed to appreciate the real reason behind Valley's tardiness, as it appeared to him, in operating the all-important floodlight.

Meanwhile, at the Newborough site, on duty that evening were LACs Leaversuch and Morris. There should have been three men present but the third, Corporal Barfield, felt ill and had decided to remain in his billet. Sitting inside their shelter the two airmen quietly passed the long hours by chatting and drinking tea. Their undemanding job was, to use RAF parlance, something of a 'cushy' number, though the total lack of activity could be oppressively tedious at times. Indeed it was true to say that nothing had ever happened at the site since it was built and the two friends had every expectation this particular night would be exactly the same as all the previous ones, but they were soon to be proved wrong.

Just after 11.00 p.m. they heard the sound of a rapidly approaching aircraft. As this was most unusual Jack Leaversuch went outside to investigate, heedless of the physical danger he might face should the unexpected visitor turn out to be an enemy raider. Climbing the small tower on top of the shelter he peered into the gloom beyond and was perturbed to see the vague outline of an aircraft flying towards him at little more than ground level.

'By God, he's low!' he shouted to his colleague and then, a split second later realised, to his horror, the aircraft was about to attempt a landing on the dummy runway. Frantically he flashed

34

the small searchlight mounted on the tower, hoping the pilot would realise his error at the last minute, but it was far too late to avert disaster. During its last moments the doomed Beaufighter was so low as it passed over Leaversuch that, in his own words, it seemed he 'Could have raised a hand and touched it.' Almost immediately afterwards the aircraft collided with the top of a 30 foot high sand dune, disintegrating in the process and bursting into flames.

With hearts pounding Leaversuch and Morris rushed to the wreckage and tried to put out the flames using two pitifully inadequate hand held extinquishers — all that was available at the 'Q' site. Faced with these difficulties, which were further aggravated by ammunition from the Beaufighter's guns exploding in the fierce heat, quenching the fire was a hopeless fight against overwhelming odds for the two airmen. Defeated by the severity of the blaze they were forced to stand and watch helplessly as the wreckage continued to burn. There was no possibility whatsoever of rescuing the aircraft's crew. When the flames eventually died down, the body of Sergeant Scott could be seen, still in an upright position, in what was left of the cockpit while Sergeant Wood's body lay on the ground nearby. Both bodies were badly burnt.

Leaversuch, in a state of shock after the events of the past few minutes, then telephoned Valley to inform the authorities of the accident. Soon a salvage party would be on its way but the first outsider to arrive was Owen Pritchard, who was in charge of the local Royal Observer Corps post, also situated in Newborough Warren's sand dunes. Thinking the crash might be that of an enemy aircraft attacking the 'Q' site, he came running up, shouting excitedly 'Is it a German, is it a German?!' Later the police arrived, as did the RAF, whose first job was to remove the bodies of Scott and Wood. They were buried in Maeshyfryd Cemetery, Holyhead, a few days later.

One of 456 Squadron's groundcrew kept a diary in which he laconically refers to the crash as follows; 'Thursday, 8th October. Five letters from home. Plenty of work. Tonight at 11.00 another Beau[fighter] cracked up, (engine failure). Both chaps killed, (pilot Scotty). Went to pictures.
'Wednesday, 14th October. Funeral today at Holyhead. All Aussies turned out and we had quite an impressive ceremony.

Three more parcels from home. Plenty of work. General panic for new kite mods. Had a good supper at night in hut.'

After an investigation into the crash it was established that Scott, in his haste, had made the final approach to the dummy flarepath at an angle of almost 90° before rounding out for the landing and so he would not have seen the screened bar of red lights, visible only from an angle of 30° or less to the runway axis. Thus a vital warning, which might have saved the Beaufighter, was missed.

Although the story is a tragic one, it does, however, possess a humorous tailpiece, well worth relating. Among the men gathering at the crash site was a policeman, a member of the Anglesey Constabulary, and a man not averse to breaking the law when it suited him. Perhaps it is better not to reveal his identity but simply to call him P.C. X. When sifting through the crash debris he found one of the aircraft's wing tanks some distance away from the main wreckage. The tank was relatively undamaged and still had fuel in it. This discovery and the prospect of obtaining a few gallons of free petrol was so tempting that P.C. X decided to steal the tank. It was therefore hidden by him in the soft sand, to be recovered later.

Some days afterwards, when the 'Q' site was back to normal, the tank was quietly removed in the dead of night and taken to a farm a few miles away. The farm belonged to a friend of the policeman and there the job began of transferring the fuel, amounting to almost 45 gallons, into a multitude of containers — cans, drums, jars etc. These containers were then carefully hidden in the farm's outbuildings and fields, eventually to be shared between the two men.

P.C. X owned an Austin 7 motor car and was keen to make us of his newly found fuel source at the first opportunity. He decided to take his wife on a trip to Llandudno and so the car's tank was filled with fuel from the crashed Beaufighter despite advice from P.C. X's friend that high octane aviation fuel was not very suitable for the car's engine. Indeed, there was every possibility that damage would ensue, though mixing oil with the fuel might help to reduce this risk. But the advice went unheeded.

On the journey to Llandudno the little Austin's performance proved to be spectacular, much to the delight of its owner. However, the return journey was very different. Trouble began when the engine refused to start. Eventually it fired and burst into life but only after much expenditure of energy with the cranking handle, together with a great deal of cursing. After driving a few miles P.C. X became aware that his car was losing power — a condition which seemed to be getting steadily worse as the journey proceeded. By the time the Austin had reached Penmaenmawr, quantities of blue smoke were coming from the exhaust. There was no doubt about it, something was seriously wrong. Soon, a lower gear had to be selected and when Anglesey was reached, the car was incapable of anything better than a 15mph crawl in low gear. Upon inspection the engine was found to have suffered major damage, with burnt out valves and badly scored cylinder walls. Such was the price the erring policeman had to pay for his misdeeds!

After the Beaufighter crash, Newborough Warren 'Q' site continued to operate until November 1943 when it was abandoned as no longer serving any useful purpose. For the next half century the ruins of the Anderson shelter remained more or less undisturbed, and was a small but powerful reminder of the War and its influence on local aviation to those that knew the building's history, until the structure was sealed up and buried under tons of sand by the Forestry Commission in the Spring of 1992.

Chapter 5

'Mountains, Leutnant!'

Flying in a mountainous region is always risky. Cliffs and steep slopes preclude an emergency landing, strong air currents abound and summits are often shrouded by clouds. It is an environment which the aviator has to treat with the greatest respect and constant alertness is called for. When something goes wrong and an accident happens, the result is fatal generally speaking. But not in every case. Sometimes, if an aircraft makes contact with the ground at an angle which approximates to that of the mountain slope then the result, provided there are no obstacles such as boulders or rocky outcrops, will be more like a belly landing than a crash, and with correspondingly higher chances of survival for the machine's occupants.

This was the fate of a German bomber which came to grief in the hills of Snowdonia during the early hours of 14 April 1941. Because three out of the four crew members survived, it has been possible to piece together a detailed, first-hand account of the flight and its unexpected sequel nearly half a century later.

The story begins at a German occupied airfield near Nantes, in northern France, where the 3rd Staffel of K.G.28 — a Luftwaffe unit whose main task was the mining of British coastal waters — was based. On 13 April one of the unit's crews was briefed to carry out an attack that night on the Royal Navy's aircraft carrier *Victorious*, which was in the Vickers-Armstrong shipyard at Barrow-in-Furness. The ship's presence had been established after a reconnaissance flight on the previous day. At dusk the four crewmen climbed aboard their aircraft, a Heinkel HE III (coded 1T+EL), which had been loaded with armour piercing bombs in readiness for the attack. The four men, now preparing to fly deep into enemy territory, were: Leutnant Lothar Horras, 21 years old, the pilot and captain (his rank being equivalent to that of a Flying Officer in the RAF), Feltwebel (Sergeant) Bruno Perzanowski, 29, the observer/bomb aimer (and a fanatical Nazi who had been awarded the Iron Cross, First Class, for service with the Kondor

Legion at the time of the Spanish Civil War), Gefreiter Kurt Schlender, 22, wireless operator and Gefreiter Josef Brüninghausen, 19, the flight engineer. His and Schlender's rank was approximately equivalent to that of an Aircraftsman I in the RAF.

After becoming airborne, the Heinkel crossed the French coast at St Malo and then took an over-water route: the English Channel, St George's Channel and the Irish Sea, before turning east for the English coast and Barrow. The flight was straightforward and without incident, though tension increased markedly inside the bomber as the moment for action drew closer.

Once over the port, Horras and his crew rapidly found the area where the aircraft carrier should have been, according to the intelligence report — but the ship was not there. Wisely, as it turned out, she was moved to another dock as a precautionary measure following the previous day's reconnaissance flight. Unable to locate their prime target, the Heinkel's disappointed crew chose, as an alternative, a target of opportunity — some harbour installations — upon which they proceeded to drop their bombs. None of the men knew it at the time, but this would be their last act of belligerence during the war. Seconds after the bombs were released, however, the *Victorious* was spotted but by then it was too late, of course, much to everyone's chagrin.

Meanwhile, ground defences had sprung into action and were directing very heavy, and accurate, anti-aircraft fire at the bomber. On board, disappointment quickly turned to consternation as explosions from bursting shells shook the aircraft violently, causing damage to the radio, flight instruments, compass, auto-pilot and blowing out some of the many perspex panels which formed the glazed front section of the machine. Leutnant Horras prudently decided to withdraw with all possible haste. He flew out over the sea before taking stock of the situation; luckily the engines were still running smoothly and so there was a good chance of reaching base, he concluded. But which was the best route to take, under the circumstances? The shortest and least time-consuming passage was a direct flight across England, but the likelihood of being intercepted by RAF fighters was regarded as almost inevitable. It was far safer to follow a longer, more circuitous path by skirting the British coastline. Here, the risk was that of running out of fuel and being forced to ditch in the sea. This seemed preferable, however, to being shot down by a Spitfire or Hurricane. Horras had also considered heading for Eire (which was a neutral country) should the engines start to give trouble, but as they were performing normally, he decided to postpone the final decision on which direction to take until the Heinkel reached Anglesey. If, by then, the engines were not running properly then he would fly towards Eire but if the two power plants continued to function well, Horras would attempt to reach base.

'We stayed low', he recollects, 'some 150-300 feet, trying to get close to the coast but since our main compass was out of action and the weather continued to be quite bad, with showers and often zero visibility, I decided to gain height since I was afraid of crashing, even on the coast of Anglesey.' The aircraft climbed without difficulty and soon entered thick cloud. Presently Schlender, who possessed an altimeter, noticed the instrument was indicating a height of 3,000 feet. Up to that point, the atmosphere was quiet and calm on board as the machine's Junkers Jumo engines were running well and the crew were reasonably confident of reaching home, but unbeknown to them an insidious danger was creeping up on the bomber — a danger that would soon shatter the men's illusion of calmness.

Suddenly the intercom crackled into life and someone said: 'Did you notice anything going past just now? What was it?' Yes, Schlender, while looking through the perspex dome above his head, thought something had 'whizzed past' but he had no idea what it was. In fact, what the crew had glimpsed were the slopes of the Carneddau mountains, into which the Heinkel had drifted in the darkness and cloudy conditions.

Sitting in the draughty cockpit, Horras noticed the machine's rate of climb had unexpectedly increased far beyond the normal capability of a bomber. He realised that the aircraft was caught in the grip of a strong upward current of air. Then Brüninghausen, who was lying on the fuselage floor, must have seen the ground through the ventral turret because he shouted a warning: 'We are in the mountains, Leutnant!' They were his last words.

The Heinkel was now within feet of the earth and there followed, almost immediately, a frightening bang from somewhere in the belly of the bomber as it touched the hillside. After the impact, which had killed Brüninghausen instantly, Horras found the aircraft continued to fly but it was now caught in a powerful downcurrent of air and in spite of the throttles being opened fully, there was too much of a delay before the machine responded. The situation was very serious; 'All of a sudden it was completely dark in front of me,' Horras recollects. 'There is black and there is blacker than black. My last reaction was to grab hold of the stick and pull it right up against me.' With his heart in his mouth, the young pilot strove to gain height but his efforts were to no avail. He could not prevent the Heinkel from crashing in a kind of uphill belly landing and bursting into flames upon doing so, on the summit slopes of Llwytmor, a 2,500 foot high mountain in the Carneddau. The time was 3.00 a.m.

In the front of the aircraft, Horras and Perzanowski were thrown forward through the already damaged nose section. Both sustained injuries; the pilot had two fingers on his right hand almost completely severed by jagged metal, while the observer suffered bruising, cuts to his face and some broken ribs. Horras lost consciousness and had no idea how much time had passed before he came to. His memory is of lying on the ground, looking at flames; 'It was my aircraft burning. I couldn't get up. I saw Perzanowski coming towards me and it was he who pulled me up. He had been injured but had got his brains working more quickly than I had. I was still dazed.'

'We stayed there for a moment, then suddenly he threw me to the ground again because ammunition was now exploding. After the fire died down, we went to the wreckage and found Brüninghausen. But Schlender was missing and we could not find him. We were unable to search around because it was dark. After some time, I don't know how long, we saw someone coming up the slope towards us. We thought he was an English soldier but it was Schlender.'

The wireless operator had been sitting at his radio set located amidships when the crash happened. At first he thought the Heinkel had collided with a barrage balloon and he was just about to grab his parachute when he realised the aircraft was on the ground. Above his head, the perspex dome had disappeared most conveniently after the impact, leaving a neat, round hole through which he escaped from the wrecked machine, which was now burning fiercely. He was glad to be free of the threat posed by the devouring flames. As he graphically put it; 'I did not want to be singed like a goose!'

Believing himself to be the sole survivor, Schlender withdrew from the immediate scene of the crash and took cover behind some boulders, where he stayed, cold and uncomfortable but alert, until dawn. When there was sufficient light he began to explore the area and was surprised, and pleased, to find Horras and Perzanowski sitting near the burnt out wreckage. The three then decided what should be done. Dealing with Horras' injured hand was the first, and obvious, priority. Schlender thought the two fingers, dangling from tendons only, had to be cut off without delay — a course of action to which their unfortunate owner had no alternative but to agree. So the wireless operator deftly removed the two digits with his knife and put a bandage on the stumps. Luckily there was no infection and the wounds eventually healed perfectly.

The men's next objective was to find help. It was unlikely, they surmised, that anyone knew of their predicament because darkness and low cloud had prevented the crash from being observed. Therefore they could not expect rescuers to arrive soon. Indeed, the trio might even be stranded on this bleak hillside for days. It was evident to them that they would have to seek a way down the mountain themselves. The clear-thinking Schlender said it would be better for him to go alone while his colleagues, still in a state of shock, remained at the crash site. But the other two thought it would be preferable if all three went together. They were afraid that if left alone on the hillside help might never come. It was a nightmare they could hardly bear to contemplate.

Schlender, however, could not accept his friends' understandable desire to go with him. His concern, above all else, was for their survival and he insisted that their best chance of early rescue was not to move from their present position. Then, as he warily began his downward journey he stumbled across the body of the fourth crew member, Brüninghausen. He noted the look of peace on the dead man's face. As mentioned previously, Brüninghausen had been lying on the Heinkel's floor at the time of the first impact, which had ripped out the lower half of the fuselage, killing the unlucky flight engineer in an instant.

Schlender continued, in the grey light of a wet, misty morning, to make good progress and, 'by an incredible stroke of luck', he said, 'I found the right way down.' Descending steadily, and treating every step with caution, he presently came across a wooded valley at the bottom of which he could see a small river and beyond that, nestling among the trees, a solitary cottage with smoke rising from the chimney. A huge surge of relief swept through his body at the sight of this lone dwelling-place. 'Where there is smoke, there must be people', he reasoned, and made a beeline for the cottage, his burden of worry already lightened by the knowledge that help would soon be available for his injured friends.

Blocking his advance towards rescue was the river but as it was neither particularly wide or deep it presented only a minor obstacle, easily overcome. After wading through the water, Schlender climbed the few yards of steep ground that separated him from his goal. Upon reaching the building he knocked firmly on the door, having taken the precaution, before doing so, of throwing away the pistol he normally carried, as he did not want to appear overly aggressive to whoever would answer his knock. He knew that any show of hostility was completely futile and his only thought was of co-operating fully with the British. There was little point in doing anything else because he was well aware that from the moment of being stranded on the mountainside, he and his companions were 'in the bag' — the airman's term for being taken prisoner. In other words, the three Germans were destined to become PoWs, spending the remainder of the war behind the wire fence of an internment camp.

But where exactly was the cottage in front of which a somewhat bedraggled Schlender now found himself standing? Although he could not have known it, he was in the upper part of the picturesque Aber Valley, 1½ miles from the village of Abergwyngregyn. The cottage, named 'Cydgoed', was occupied by a married couple, the Baxters, and it was Mrs Baxter who came to the door. She had been preparing breakfast when she heard Schlender's insistent tapping. Assuming that the early morning visitor (the time was 7.20 a.m.) was the postman, she opened the door unhesitatingly. But to the housewife's utter astonishment, instead of the letter-carrier with his usual cheery greetings, there stood a rather wet and dishevelled looking man dressed in German military uniform. Speaking in halting, broken English he managed to inform the astounded Mrs Baxter that he was an airman whose aircraft had crashed and that help was needed. Recovering from her surprise, she invited him in for a cup of tea!

Then, while she went to telephone the authorities, her husband took charge of the unexpected guest, and after a short while the local police and members of the Home Guard arrived. Schlender remembers with amusement the reaction of one Home Guard soldier in particular: 'First I saw a rifle with a bayonet being pushed through the opening crack of the door, then there was a head with a round tin hat; a Tommy. He looked around, gave me a friendly smile and said: ' ''Where is the German?'' ' He looked again, realised that it was me, placed his rifle in the corner, came up to me and said: ' ''Shake hands!'' ' It was really nice. He was so taken aback to find one of the bad Nazis, he'd quite lost his nerve.'

Soon an officer arrived at Cydgoed and proceeded to interrogate Schlender: 'Among his many questions he asked me whether I was feeling strong enough to climb back up to the crash since my comrades were still up there. I said yes, so a policeman lent me his raincoat — it was raining — and we went up again.' Meanwhile, his two companions, unable to stay on the mountainside, had started to descend and they too found the right path. Presently the rescue party, while moving upwards, came across them and as Schlender stated: 'We met Horras and Perzanowski hobbling towards us, supporting one another.' They also ended up in Mrs Baxter's kitchen, where she looked after them ' . . . with the most touching care', according to a grateful Horras.

The body of Brüninghausen had still to be recovered and so some of the party, including Schlender, continued to the crash site. It was still misty on the mountain but the wreckage was easily located because of the smell of smoke. The flight engineer's body was covered up with parachute material, put on a stretcher and brought, not without some difficulty, down to the valley.

Of the three survivors, Perzanowski, the fanatical Nazi, was the least co-operative with his captors. Imposingly tall and with an arrogant manner, he maintained a haughty aloofness, chiding the other two for being over-friendly with the British. Even expressing a simple thanks for the kindness shown to them by Mrs Baxter was frowned upon. From Aber, the Germans were taken to the hospital at Bangor, where their wounds were treated. All three were subsequently incarcerated in Prisoner of War camps located in Canada. Brüninghausen was buried at Pwllheli but in the 1950s his remains were re-interred in the German War Cemetery at Cannock, Staffordshire.

After the war ended, Horras and Schlender were repatriated to Germany, but not Perzanowski. Reference has already been made to his fanatical adherence to Nazi ideology — a fanaticism which remained undiminished throughout his captivity and which generated a passion in his breast that burned as fiercely in 1945, when Germany lay in ruins, as it did in the glory-days of 1939 and 1940 when Hitler's armies seemed invincible. It was this extreme of zealousness which led Perzanowski ultimately to a tragic end; hanging from a gallows. In September 1944, at the Canadian PoW camp known as Medicine Hat, he, and three other diehard Nazis conspired to murder a fellow German whom they accused of being a Communist, and to whom the quartet of killers did eventually deal a lethal blow. For this crime they were put on trial and after being found guilty the four were executed in December 1946.

Horras and Schlender, in complete contrast to their colleague, flourished. Putting the years of stagnation spent in Canadian internment camps behind them, they went on to build new and successful lives in a reformed, democratic West Germany, leaving once fresh memories of their crash in the Welsh mountains to fade into the dim half-light of the past.

However, the physical evidence of that traumatic event, the wrecked bomber itself, could still be seen on Llwytmor for many years after the end of the war but as time passed, the amount of wreckage left on the hillside steadily decreased, for one simple reason; the aircraft was as attractive to souvenir hunters as carrion to jackals and vultures, and with similar results — a carcass picked so clean that hardly the skeleton remained, even.

There the story would have ended, except for the television company Harlech TV and one of their producers, Michael Bayley Hughes. Thanks to him, another chapter — this time gratifyingly happy in comparison to what had gone before — was added to the story, nearly fifty years after the accident had taken place. In 1989 Bayley Hughes was hard at work making programmes for S4C, the Welsh language television channel. As someone with a considerable interest in aviation he was pleased to be producing *Adar y Ddrycin* (Birds of the Storm), a thirty minute documentary on wartime crashes in Snowdonia. The programme was designed to provide viewers with a broad picture of events, using contributions from local aviation historians and enthusiasts. In addition, it was decided that one accident should be described in more detail, to give depth and extra interest to the film. For this purpose the Heinkel's crash was chosen, primarily because research had established that Horras and Schlender were still living in Germany, and they, as survivors relating their personal experiences, would add a great deal to the impact of the programme. Then, in the course of his research Bayley Hughes discovered a fact which offered him an interesting prospect; the two Germans had been sent to different Prisoner of War camps in Canada — Horras to a camp for officers and Schlender to one for NCOs.

Since that time neither man had been in touch with, or knew the whereabouts of the other. This lack of contact gave the TV producer a marvellous opportunity to spring a surprise upon the two. Clearly, a reunion between them was essential and would form an important part of the film, but instead of this event taking place in Germany, as might have been expected, why not keep the location temporarily secret and have a much more dramatic meeting at the actual crash site itself, on Llwytmor mountain? To increase further the element of surprise why not keep Horras and Schlender in ignorance of each other's continuing existence until the moment when they would meet on the hillside? By practising a little gentle deception it would be easy to bring the two, independently of course, to Aber, where Bayley Hughes' camera crew would be waiting. The ensuing meeting, he hoped, would provide some good material for his film. In the event, he was not to be disappointed.

Thus, early in August 1989 after filming had taken place in Germany, the two unsuspecting men arriving in North Wales where, they were told, further filming would be carried out at the crash site. They stayed at different hotels, many miles apart and on the appointed day, 4 August, both were preparing for a return to the mountain slopes where they had last stood nearly half a century ago. Each, believing he was the only survivor present, had been

46

briefed that an interview would take place, at which the services of a German interpreter would be available in case of language difficulties. Thus the trap was laid.

Friday the 4th turned out to be an excellent day for filming. The weather, in keeping with the hot summer experienced that year, was truly superb: warm sunshine, clear blue skies, unlimited visibility and little or no wind. There would be few technical problems for the film crew, who had been airlifted by helicopter to Llwytmor. On the mountainside, a slightly apprehensive Bayley Hughes, unsure as to exactly what would happen when his 'victims' met, prepared to record the scene. Then the moment came; Horras, 69 years old and Schlender, 70, were face to face on the piece of ground where they had last stood, as young men, in 1941.

After a brief interchange in German between the pair, there was a lengthy pause as the truth slowly dawned upon them. When recognition came, they responded with a warmth which showed that a gap of four decades had not weakened in the least the camaraderie that existed between the two. For Schlender in particular, emotions aroused by the meeting proved so strong that tears filled his eyes as he greeted his friend. Hardly able to believe what had happened, he took hold of Horras' right hand and checked how many fingers he had. 'Yes, look — that's what happened to my hand', said Horras, revealing that two of his fingers were missing. This was final and indisputable proof to Schlender that the person standing before him was indeed none other than his wartime comrade of old!

Michael Bayley Hughes, for his part, felt more than satisfied with the outcome of his plans. The reunion had furnished him with exactly the kind of material that he had hoped for and he knew the scene would make good viewing when *Adar y Ddrycin* came to be transmitted, (on 11 April 1990). As had been anticipated, the programme proved to be thoroughly entertaining and informative.

Before leaving for home, the two Germans travelled to the war cemetery at Cannock to see the grave of their dead colleague, Brüninghausen. Horras, remarking on the fact that most of his friends in the Luftwaffe had been killed in the war, observed that this would have been his fate also, except for the crash at Aber. Though it seemed a disaster at the time, in reality it was a piece of good fortune which probably saved him from a much worse fate if he had continued to take part in hostilities. One thing was abundantly clear to all who met him, and Schlender, during their visit to North Wales; the men's warmth and friendliness (fully reciprocated by their hosts, one has to say) indicated that old enmities, once so destructively potent, had happily disappeared forever into the past.

Chapter 6

RAF Llandwrog's Worst Crash

During the war one of Llandwrog's prime tasks was the training of air gunners. From July 1941 until the station's closure in June 1945 a steady stream of young men arrived here in order to learn the techniques of aerial gunnery. After a course of instruction lasting two months or so the successful ones were awarded their flying brevet and sergeants stripes before moving on to OTUs for further training, to be followed by a posting to an operational squadron, usually in Bomber Command.

The training unit at Llandwrog in 1941 was No. 9 Air Gunnery School, equipped with twelve Armstrong Whitworth Whitley aircraft and a similar number of Westland Lysanders. The Whitley bomber had seen front line service during the early part of the war, had been relegated to OTUs, from where the aircraft were now being handed down, in a somewhat battered state, to Air Gunnery Schools such as the one at Llandwrog.

In order to carry out the aerial part of their training, the pupil gunners, five or six at a time, would fly in a Whitley, with each man taking turns to fire the aircraft's guns at drogue targets towed by Lysanders. Practice firings would take place over Caernarfon Bay, and the lumbering, obsolescent Whitleys, with their characteristic nose-down attitude, soon became a familiar sight in the area. The type was also flown from RAF Penrhos, near Pwllheli, on similar duties.

Invariably, some were lost in accidents: K7242 in June 1941, for example, and T4153 during the following month but the most serious loss of all occurred in October 1941 as the result of a mid-air collision. Indeed, it was the worst crash to take place at any of Gwynedd's wartime airfields.

In the early afternoon of Friday 10 October two Whitleys, K7252 and K9041, were being prepared for training flights. Piloting K7252 was Squadron Leader H. Barker, who held the post of Officer Commanding, Flying (i.e. the person in charge of all flying activity — one of the most responsible and important jobs at any RAF operational station) while the other aircraft was to be flown by a staff pilot, Flight Lieutenant E. Martin. At 2.00 p.m. six pupils, accompanied by a gunnery instructor and a civilian air mechanic, entered Squadron Leader Barker's aircraft at the same time as another group of six pupils and their instructors climbed aboard Flight Lieutenant Martin's machine. Take off was shortly afterwards: K7252 at 2.10 p.m. and K9041 at 2.15 p.m.

For the next hour they continued normally with their flights, then at 3.15 p.m. Squadron Leader Barker's aircraft returned to the airfield and joined the circuit on an approach to land on the east-west runway. A few moments later Flight Lieutenant Martin also returned and prepared to land on the same runway, but without doing a circuit — an omission from normal flying procedure which is always potentially dangerous. In this particular case the danger was very real. As Martin turned to port and levelled out for the landing, he was unaware of the other Whitley, with which he was now on a collision course.

However, at the last moment both pilots saw each other and took avoiding action but it was too late. The aircraft collided, fell to the ground, and erupted into a huge fireball which was seen from Anglesey, some two miles away across the waters of the Menai Strait. Seventeen men perished in the flames.

Three of Llandwrog's pilots saw the disaster taking place and their testimony provides a graphic account of that afternoon's events. First, Flight Lieutenant M. Holmes, the officer in charge of the target towing flight: 'At 3.15 p.m. I had just landed on the east-west runway,' he states, 'and was standing in my Lysander aircraft ready to get out when I saw two Whitley aircraft coming in to land. I had seen Squadron Leader Barker make a wide circuit of the aerodrome and he was making a long low approach in the yellow* Whitley. I saw the black* Whitley make an approach without doing a circuit, turning to port all the time. After levelling out at about 200 feet it was almost immediately below Squadron Leader Barker's aircraft. I think Flight Lieutenant Martin saw the other Whitley for the first time, slightly above him. He tried to avoid a collision by turning away to port but his starboard propeller cut off the other aircraft's tailplane. This Whitley then turned on

---

* Presumably K7252 had received the yellow paint scheme applied to training aircraft while K9041 had not.

its back and went straight into the ground, bursting into flames on impact. It was impossible to get near the blazing wreckage.'

The tailplane had fallen about fifty yards from the main wreckage. Flight Lieutenant Holmes then described what happened to K9041: 'It began to swing to port, dropping its starboard wing, hitting the ground just at the commencement of what looked like a spin and burst into flames on impact.'

The second eye witness was another of Llandwrog's staff pilots, Pilot Officer W. Adams. When the accident happened he was standing 200 yards north of the runway on which the aircraft were landing. He saw Squadron Leader Barker make a normal approach at about 100 feet. Then, he states: 'I saw a black Whitley coming in to land from a steep gliding turn at a height of 600 feet. From the position of this machine no one in it could possibly see the other aircraft.' Adams described how both machines came down to the same level after which both pilots must have seen each other because, 'Squadron Leader Barker started turning right and Flight Lieutenant Martin banked to the left but the starboard propeller of his aircraft cut the tail assembly clean off the other Whitley. This machine turned to port upside down and dived straight to the ground, bursting into flames on impact. Martin's aircraft made a turn and I could see that his starboard wing was damaged and sagging, with both motors opened full out. He was losing height and obviously was going to crash. At the time of impact I was about fifty yards away.'

The Whitley's starboard wing hit first and was crushed, the machine then went on its back, while the tail broke off before flames engulfed the aircraft. Pilot Officer Adams made a brave attempt at rescue: 'I got to within ten yards, down wind,' he states, 'but as my face was singeing I had to get back. I saw three bodies on the upwind side of the aircraft but it was obvious they were dead. Flight Lieutenant Martin was lying some twenty feet from the wreckage and was alive when I got to him.' Sadly, he was so badly burnt that he died an hour later.

The third eye witness was Pilot Officer Watson, who was due to fly K9041 on another training flight at 3.20 p.m. While crossing the airfield towards the Flight Office he watched the two aircraft above. 'I saw Squadron Leader Barker do a full circuit of the aerodrome,' he writes, 'and make a normal approach in Whitley

7252. As I moved across the aerodrome my view was obscured by a hangar and Squadron Leader Barker's aircraft sank below my line of vision. I then saw the other aircraft do a fairly steep turn and also disappear behind the hangar. I guessed they were going to collide.'

Anticipating the crash, Pilot Officer Watson started to run. His first view was of K7252 hitting the ground and bursting into flames. As for Flight Lieutenant Martin's aircraft: 'it seemed to accelerate upwards and forwards, obviously with the motors wide open and climbing fast. The starboard wing and propeller were obviously damaged. She started to turn to starboard, out of control, and turn almost vertically and hit the ground, immediately bursting into flames. I had been running towards where I thought the aircraft were going to crash and reached there just after Pilot Officer Adams.' However, there was nothing either man could do to assist the victims of what was Gwynedd's worst mid-air collision. In the space of a few seconds RAF Llandwrog lost two pilots, one of whom was the most senior on the station, two gunnery instructors, twelve air gunner trainees and a civilian mechanic. It was a tragic loss.

Because of wartime censorship imposed upon newspapers, this accident, in common with the vast majority of others, was not reported in the local press and thus the populance at large remained in ignorance of events, but after a crash of this magnitude it was virtually impossible to prevent word from spreading, especially within the immediate locality. Soon, rumours were rife in Llandwrog village — rumours that quickly came to the ears of the local policeman, who had not been told of the accident. He regarded this omission as a serious matter which called for an explanation, and so, in high dudgeon he, together with a colleague to provide moral support, went to the airfield and demanded to see the station commander, Wing Commander Bruce.

He readily agreed to meet the policemen but when face to face with them his expectation of a reasonable talk were dashed as he found himself being rebuked in no uncertain manner for his alleged neglect of duty. It was the Wing Commander's responsibility, he was told, to inform the police immediately of any fatal accident as the police were the agents of the Coroner. Furthermore, as this was a requirement dictated by law, the RAF had a legal obligation, therefore, to impart information to the police.

The station commander could easily have adopted a conciliatory approach to his accuser, placating him with a mild apology, but Bruce was not in that frame of mind. He replied in the strongest terms that he was far too busy writing to bereaved families and the Air Ministry to bother about informing the police. Having to write even one letter to next-of-kin was distressing enough, he said, but writing to seventeen was infinitely more so. In addition, as the accident happened on the airfield, in his view, it was an internal matter for the RAF only. This had the effect of infuriating the policemen and tempers flared, though all parties in the argument managed to restrain themselves sufficiently to maintain decorum. In the end, the village constable and his colleague were forced to depart without obtaining much satisfaction, but at least a protest had been made.

As noted, the collision of the two Whitleys resulted in a fire seen by people in Anglesey. Among these was a middle aged farmer working on that Friday afternoon in one of his fields, close to the shoreline at Abermenai point. Watching the flames and smoke, he surmised, correctly, there had been an accident but with a veil of secrecy drawn around all local military activity he heard no more about the crash and as time passed the unexplained event faded into the recess of his memory. There it remained for forty years, until 1981, when, quite by chance, he, now in his old age, met the author and a discussion on life in wartime Anglesey ensued, including the story of the mystery fire seen at Llandwrog, for which, of course, the author was more than pleased to provide an explanation to a somewhat surprised farmer.

Chapter 7

The Brief Life of *Bachelors' Baby*

On Monday 3rd January 1944, in the dreary gloom of a mid-winter day an American B-24 Liberator landed at RAF Valley, Anglesey, after a flight from the warmer climes of North Africa — the Moroccan city of Marrakesh, to be precise.

As the aircraft rolled along the runway with decreasing speed and turned on to a taxi-track, the crew noticed that the weather was deteriorating almost by the minute as drizzle and low cloud moved in to blanket the area. For the B-24's ten occupants it seemed that even before they had properly set foot on British soil they were getting a taste of the grey, damp conditions that were such a dispiriting feature of the climate at that time of year. The arrival of the Liberator was by no means an isolated incident. On the contrary, the aircraft was one of scores — some 250 bombers during the previous six months — which had crossed the Atlantic ocean in order to participate in the air war against Germany. This aerial armada, comprised mostly of B-17 Flying Fortresses and B-24 Liberators belonging to the American 8th Air Force utilised long and somewhat circuitous routes to reach Valley before embarking on a final hop to operational airfields, usually in East Anglia.

Indeed, as a result of this inward flow, Valley had been transformed from a relatively minor RAF fighter station to an important trans-Atlantic terminal used by ever increasing numbers of American bombers. While the vast majority of these aircraft reached their destinations within the UK in safety, a few did not, amongst them the B-24 which had touched down at Valley on that particular Monday.

Although greeted by dismal weather on their arrival, the crew nevertheless remained in good spirits. They were nearly at the end of their lengthy journey and would, they assumed, soon be given the opportunity to fly operational bombing missions against targets in Germany. For ten young men thirsting for adventure, the chance of action was a heady, exciting prospect. Their destiny, however, was to be very different. Delayed at fog-bound Valley for a few days, the Liberator, within half an hour of becoming airborne was to end up as nothing more than a burning wreck on a Welsh hillside, with five of the crew dead or dying and all the others suffering some degree of injury.

The men were led by 26 year old 2nd Lt. Adrian (or Ace as he was known) Schultz, the aircraft's pilot. Under his command he had: 2nd Lt. Art Davis, co-pilot, 2nd Lt. Jules Ertz, navigator, 2nd Lt. Norman Boyer, bomb-aimer, Staff Sergeant Sammy Offutt, flight engineer, Staff Sergeant John Tymczak, radio operator and four air gunners: Sergeants Joe Neiglos, Harold Alexander, Bill Lorenz and Bill Nichols.

In civilian life Ace Schultz had earned his living as a salesman with a photographic company in the mid-west city of Omaha but in October 1941 he gave up his job and enrolled in the Army Air Corps. For twelve months he worked as an aircraft technician before deciding to apply for pilot training — a logical step for him, now that America was in the war and there was a demand for aircrew. His application was successful and so Schultz became a cadet pilot, swapping his rather routine ground job for the much more glamorous and demanding business of learning to fly. After gaining his wings in May 1943, he was commissioned as a 2nd Lieutenant. He then embarked on a heavy bomber combat training course, during which the aforementioned nine-man crew was assigned to him. Henceforth they would fly together as a team.

Early in November 1943, with their training completed, Schultz and his crew were sent to Herington Field, Texas, where they picked up the machine they would subsequently operate: a brand-new B-24J Liberator, serial number 42-99991. In common with all other bomber crews, Schultz's men personalised their aircraft with a name, and had the nose section of the B-24's fuselage decorated with a painting. Many aircraft paintings had an erotic element — usually depicting a scantily clad, curvaceous female in a suggestive pose — a style which the crew of 42-99991 wholeheartedly followed. Embellishing the front of their B-24 was a voluptuous blonde, naked except for a baby's nappy fastened by an oversize safety pin. In one hand the blonde had a bottle of champagne and in the other a raised glass. Emblazoned underneath in large letters was the aircraft's name: *Bachelors' Baby*

— chosen by the crew to reflect the fact that they were all unmarried.

Time was spent at Herington testing and fitting out the new machine in preparation for the operational flying still to come. It was also during this period that *Bachelors' Baby* acquired an extra, though unofficial, crew member — a six weeks old black and white fox terrier puppy, which the crew had taken on board as a pet. The dog displayed supercharged energy and was named Booster after the engine superchargers, which were known as boosters. Furthermore, as Schultz observed to his satisfaction, the animal gave a huge boost to crew morale, so the choice of name was particularly apt.

After Herington, the Liberator was flown to Morrison Field near Palm Beach, Florida, where other bombers were amassing in readiness for departure to various theatres of war, either in Europe, North Africa or the Far East. The final destination of each bomber was highly classified information withheld even from the individual aircraft commanders. Therefore, when *Bachelors' Baby* rose into the Florida skies on 15 December 1943 none on board knew with any degree of certainty where they were going. That information was carried by Schultz in a sealed packet of orders marked 'Secret', which he was instructed to open only after flying on a general heading out to sea for a distance of two hundred miles from Morrison.

As can be imagined, the contents of this packet caused much speculation amongst the crew, all of whom hoped that Europe would be their ultimate destination, and so when the time came for Schultz to break the seal and read out the orders over the aircraft's inter-com, his words were listened to with the keenest interest. When he announced that Britain was to be their goal a huge cheer of approval went up from the men.

The B-24 would not be part of a group for the long journey ahead; rather, she would fly alone, with her commander granted the freedom to make up his own flight plans, though within the confines of a well-established path known as the Southern Overseas Route, which took American aircraft to Europe by way of airfields in the Carribean, South America and North Africa. A period of thirty days was allowed for the flight, which may seem over-generous but the crew had to carry out a certain amount of anti-submarine patrols (U-boats were quite active in the Caribbean and South Atlantic during this period) as well as perform their own maintenance work on the aircraft whilst en route.

Before leaving Morrison, the Liberator's bomb-bay, like all other departing aircraft, was loaded with a cargo of much needed aero-engine spares and aircraft equipment for eventual delivery to US depots in Britain. This was an obvious and most convenient method of ferrying war material across the Atlantic by utilising space within the B-17s and B-24s which would otherwise be wasted. Unfortunately however, *Bachelors' Baby* had been loaded without sufficient care being given to the even distribution of weight within the bomb-bay, with the result that on becoming airborne, the aircraft was impossible to trim properly, thus imposing a rather heavy work load on the two pilots, who had to fly their machine with more physical effort than would normally have been the case. It was a problem which was to plague them all the way to Anglesey.

Their first stop was at Borinquen in Puerto Rico, followed by Waller Field on the island of Trinidad, and then a flight along the coast of South America to Belem and Natal, where an attempt to redistribute the freight more evenly was made by so-called loading experts whose efforts, in the event, served only to compound rather than alleviate the difficulties.

On Christmas Eve the Liberator departed from Natal on the longest leg of the trip — nearly 2,500 miles of over-water flying to Dakar, in West Africa. It turned out to be a thoroughly unpleasant flight which nearly ended in disaster. Not only did Schultz and Davis have their hands full fighting to keep their unbalanced aircraft on an even keel but in mid-ocean they encountered a severe tropical storm which blew them badly off course. The eleven hours scheduled for the crossing stretched into thirteen long, exhausting ones, filled with anxiety, before Dakar was sighted by a hugely relieved crew. The B-24 landed with only two of its engines providing power, the other two having been stopped so as to conserve fuel. Indeed, with the cockpit gauges showing 'empty' and only a few gallons left in the tanks, the lack of fuel was so critical that *Bachelors' Baby* could have remained airborne for only another few minutes. It had been a close shave.

The crew remained overnight at Dakar before setting off in the morning for Marrakesh, having taken the opportunity before doing so, of shifting the cargo yet again in the hope of curing the trim problem, but there was only a minor improvement during the flight. At Marrakesh, aircraft loading specialists were asked to look at the B-24's load, which they did, and then proceeded to completely change its distribution within the bomb-bay. This seemed to have the desired effect on the Liberator's handling characteristics, which were noticably better at the start of the next stage — the flight that would bring *Bachelors' Baby* to Valley. Then as the journey progressed, the problem which had so bedevilled Schultz and his co-pilot since they had left the United States slowly but surely reappeared. Most probably, changing the cargo around had caused the centre of gravity to move, though the troublesome effects this gave rise to were partially obscured, initially, by the weight of a full fuel load in the B-24's tanks. But as the fuel was progressively used up, the load lightened, thus allowing the change in the centre of gravity to manifest itself.

Unable to trim their aircraft properly, the pilot and co-pilot had little option but to remain flying in an untrimmed condition during the latter half of their flight to Anglesey, where, as already noted, they landed without further incident. In the course of that first evening at Valley, Schultz, Davis and Sammy Offutt made a thorough inspection of the Liberator and found a small amount of slack in the control cables. It was not a serious fault — just a slight lack of tension which had been sufficient to impart a somewhat mushy feel to the controls. As the bomber was now only a short hop from its final destination, Schultz decided that no remedial action was necessary, either to tighten the control cables or adjust the bomb-bay load. He would tolerate the situation until he reached his new base.

In addition to the legitimate freight within the Liberator's belly there was a fair amount of contraband also — chocolates, cigarettes, perfume, silk stockings, lipstick and fine fabrics, for example. Such items, though plentiful enough in the United States, were not so in the conditions of austerity and rationing prevalent in wartime Britain. The crew of *Bachelors' Baby*, like all American servicemen entering the country, knew that a supply of these highly desirable luxuries could considerably increase their chances of success with the opposite sex and so the men had made sure of their quota, ready to tempt the ladies whenever an opportunity arose!

Schultz and his crew expected their stay at Valley to be brief, as transatlantic arrivals rarely remained longer than 24 hours. The vast majority would depart after an overnight stop and to this end a smooth running, efficient organisation had been built up to deal with incoming aircraft as quickly as possible before sending them on to other UK destinations. When disruption and delay occurred, however, the most frequent culprit was bad weather, which as we have seen, followed closely on the heels of *Bachelors' Baby*. Soon after the bomber landed, conditions deteriorated to such an extent that flying was not possible and the airfield's operational effectiveness, consequently, was reduced to almost nil.

But if the Liberator's crew thought that the drizzle and lowering cloudbase which had greeted them would soon dispel, they were wrong. It was, in fact, the start of a prolonged period of bad weather. For three tedious, oppressive days conditions remained unchanged, forcing an irksome inactivity on many staff and breaking up the well regulated flow of arrivals and departures, including that of *Bachelors' Baby*.

One method of overcoming the problems created by this type of situation was to use an aircraft equipped with the 'Gee' navigation aid to shepherd weather-bound aircraft from Valley to their destinations. 'Gee' was a pioneer precision radio navigational system invented during the early part of the war, and which proved to be invaluable in so many circumstances, including those which now prevailed at the Anglesey airbase, where accurate route finding by departing aircraft was essential yet difficult to achieve when crews found themselves in the restrictive opacity of cloud almost as soon as they were in the air.

On Thursday 6th January, with *Bachelors' Baby* and six other B-24s grounded since the 3rd, and with only a slight improvement in the weather, a B-17 Flying Fortress fitted with a 'G-box', as the Americans called it, arrived to act as a shepherd for the group on the final leg of their journey, which in this case was due to end at the US 8th Air Force's depot at Watton, deep in the East Anglian countryside some twenty miles from Norwich.

In marginal conditions — low, scudding cloud, poor visibility, mist and drizzle — the flight prepared for take-off. Of the seven bombers, Schultz's was the last to leave the dispersal point, but his aircraft made little progress. Shortly after starting to taxi, he was instructed to return to the Operations section in order to pick up Technical Sergeant Cennemo, a crew member from one of the other B-24s who had negligently misplaced some equipment and in consequence missed his flight while searching for the lost items. But no sooner had the tardy airman, whose carelessness was to cost him his life, climbed aboard when a further order came through; *Bachelors' Baby* had to remain where it was and could not rejoin the rest of the group. The weather was worsening with such rapidity that the other B-24s could not be delayed a moment longer, waiting for Schultz to catch up, otherwise the opportunity to become airborne would be lost.

All six Liberators got away safely, leaving the somewhat despairing crew of the seventh with the prospect of yet one more day at Valley, hoping the morrow would bring better weather, but in the event, the hoped for improvement failed to materialise. If anything, the situation was worse — an extremely low cloud base, intermittent rain and thick patches of mist rolling in from the sea. The airfield, bleak and cold at the best of times, was particularly so when caught in a seemingly endless bout of winter weather. To escape from this dreariness some of the B-24's crew spent the night in Bangor sampling the local beer and other delights. By mid-morning all were back on the airfield waiting for the B-17 shepherd, which it had been made known, would return that day, bad weather or not.

This aircraft duly arrived in the early afternoon, when conditions were as marginal for flying as they had been during the previous few days. While the B-17 circled overhead, Schultz received orders to take-off immediately because even worse weather was imminent. At 1.45 p.m. the long-delayed bomber finally became airborne but unfortunately soon ran into trouble. From the moment when the safety of the ground was exchanged for the uncertainties of the air, problems began to accumulate for the aircraft's crew — the principal difficulty being that of keeping up with the lead B-17 so as to remain in visual contact. Schultz, in his attempts to keep the leader in sight was seriously handicapped, not only by the all-enveloping gloom of low cloud down to 200 feet but even more so by the fact that *Bachelors' Baby* was crammed with cargo almost to the point of excess, thus making the heavily burdened Liberator sluggish in her response to any increase in power settings.

The B-17, on the other hand, was not carrying any load at all and was therefore much more fleet than its rather ponderous companion. Schultz made repeated requests to the other pilot to reduce his speed but at no time could the B-24 get any closer than a quarter of a mile to the Fortress. With a lighter load and in clearer air formating on the leader would have been simple and straightforward; now, in an unresponsive aircraft lumbering along underneath a cloudbase of only 200 feet, it became a severe test of flying skill.

The escort aircraft, as it headed away from Valley, apparently intended to steer a course of 080°, which would have taken it and *Bachelors' Baby* across Anglesey before they would have crossed the island's coast at Red Wharf Bay and then proceeded to fly some miles out to sea on an approximately parallel line to the North Wales coast, with Rhyl and Chester being the two planned waypoints before turning south east towards East Anglia. But probably because of the Liberator's difficulties in keeping station, the B-17's pilot helpfully flew a series of long elliptical orbits tracking due east across Anglesey, to give the labouring B-24 every chance to catch up. This, however, Schultz could not do. Flying at a mere 150 feet, he was forced to put his machine into almost continuous skidding intercept turns in his unsuccessful attempts to close on the lead aircraft.

This type of manouvering, carried out at little more than treetop height, was both awkward and dangerous. Skidding turns were necessary in these circumstances because it would have been far too risky to allow a wing to drop as in a normal banked turn. Even a mild degree of bank could be perilous at this altitude, as Schultz discovered when on several occasions he hastily had to lift a wing in order to clear a house or a clump of trees. Tension was further increased on the Liberator's flight deck when the gyro compass could not be set because of the never ending skidding turns and to make matters worse, the magnetic compass needle began to swing wildly. Schultz was in an unenviable position, to say the least, and one that would have caused stress to even the most phlegmatic of pilots.

Eventually the two aircraft, after crossing Anglesey more or less at nought feet, with the thunder of their engines no doubt rattling the doors and windows of many an island *tyddyn* in the process, found themselves at the northern extremity of the Menai Strait, which Schultz mistakenly took to be a river. Slipping by underneath the starboard wing he could see a sizeable town, which was, of course, Bangor. This point marked the end of the Liberator's constant manouvering. Forced down by low cloud to within a hundred feet of the sea, neither aircraft could advance at this height because of the proximity of rising ground immediately to the south. In additon, the possibility of a wingtip touching the water, with disastrous results, was very real.

Dangerously close to the Snowdonia hills and sandwiched between the sea underneath and a vast expanse of cloud above, the aircraft was caught in a blind alley from which escape was now the only remaining option. Being the leader, it was the B-17 pilot's prerogative to take action, which he promptly did. As he initiated a climbing turn to port he radioed his instructions; he was going to set a course and the Liberator was to follow closely. Nothing would have pleased Schultz more than to comply, but as we have already seen, the struggling aircraft had failed to close in on its escort since the pair's departure from Valley. In a climb, there was even less chance of doing so.

Flying over the sea, about one mile north east of Bangor, the B-24's hard-pressed pilot did his utmost to keep the Fortress in sight, half-hidden as it was in the murky greyness. A distance of approximately ¼ of a mile separated the bombers, with the B-17 flying some 30° to port of the other machine. It was at this stage that Schultz's luck ran out. Suddenly, the B-17 had gone, swallowed up completely by the mist and low cloud, the aircraft's reassuring presence vanishing within the space of a second or two. Visual contact, essential in these circumstances, had been lost, and with it the lifeline to safety. Peering through the windscreen, all Schultz could see in the distance was a barrier of ground, rising into the cloudbase.

Although it might be uncharitable and grossly unfair to suggest that it actually was the case, the Fortress pilot's actions can be interpreted as being extremely unhelpful to the hapless B-24. The pilot must surely have been aware of the difficulties experienced by the trailing aircraft, and so when he decided to climb, ordering Schultz to 'follow closely', he must have known that the Liberator, still a quarter of a mile away, could not speedily close the gap to that necessary for visual contact to be maintained in thick cloud, into which the Fortress was about to enter. Outwardly at least, it seemed like an abandonment. It was as if Schultz was being told that if he could not move in towards the B-17 quickly, then he was going to be left on his own, regardless of the consequences.

So what had caused the escort pilot to behave in such a seemingly selfish manner? Could he have felt the pressure of being hemmed in by the mist and hills so suffocating that he had to escape at all costs, allowing the instinct for self-preservation to overcome any scruples he might have had about his action? Or perhaps it was utter exasperation at the Liberator's failure to formate properly that led to a loss of patience? It is virtually impossible, at this remove, to tell what motivated the pilot's conduct during that moment. Indeed, it might be totally erroneous, as already implied, to suggest that self-preservation was the prime motivator. Schultz expresses his view of the incident succinctly and without rancour: 'He knew where he was and where he was going. I didn't. The B-17 was probably light enough to climb over the hills, but it's my guess that the pilot felt boxed in by those hills, just as I did, and he hightailed it north up Conwy Bay.'

Such a method of release from the trap was not available to the over-burdened B-24, whose pilot now had to grapple with this latest setback. He knew the Fortress could not be far but he knew also that the chance of sighting it again, in that limitless blanket of cloud was infinitesimal. Desperately he radioed his escort to say that he had lost contact, to which the peremptory reply was: 'Hold your course.' In reality, however, the Liberator at that moment was not flying on any specific compass heading; it was merely following the lead aircraft. Surrounded by dense cloud and with high ground only a few miles from his position, Schultz had to find a way out from his predicament at once, as any delay would only further endanger the aircraft. If he had continued to fly at low level in such bad conditions and when so close to mountains he was inviting nothing less than calamity.

Deliverance from the threat of complete entrapment was possible either by climbing or attempting to return to Valley by following the Anglesey coastline — an admittedly risky though not impossible avenue of escape which Schultz, probably because of his unfamiliarity with local topography, did not consider. Rather, his preferred course of action was to gain height. Calling up the B-17 he said: 'We'll climb up and meet you on top,' reasoning that if both aircraft were gaining altitude they would emerge, sooner or later, into the clear air above, where, with luck, they would make visual contact again. Extra power was fed to the B-24's engines and her nose pointed upwards in a climbing turn to the left. In no time at all she was in thick cloud. Nothing could be seen from the cockpit except a wall of greyness, as impenetrable to vision as one of bricks and mortar.

Whether or not Liberator and Fortress would have regained contact will remain a question forever unanswered because soon after starting to climb, the B-24 crashed on a hill 1,300 feet above the coastal village of Llanfairfechan. The trap which so threatened the aircraft had finally been sprung; *Bachelors' Baby* had drifted too far inland before sufficient height was gained.

What follows is a description of events occurring immediately prior to the actual impact, based on the official report, eye witness accounts and subsequent research, but a number of details, it has to be said, are disputed by a principal player in the drama — the Liberator's pilot. Therefore, his version of the crash sequence is also presented, so that the reader may judge for himself which account is likely to possess the greater authenticity.

First to realize that an accident was in the making was Llanfairfechan's policeman, P.C. W. Hughes-Parry. While working in his garden he heard the unmistakable throbbing sound of a heavy, multi-engined aircraft approaching, and upon looking up he saw the ill-fated bomber's outline emerging from the mist. To his consternation he noted how low the aircraft was flying and also the fact that it was heading towards the mountains. Convinced that a disaster was about to take place, he hurriedly telephoned the local doctor before setting off for the high ground above the village, fully prepared for whatever scene of carnage that might greet his eyes.

Aboard *Bachelors' Baby*, the terrible danger hidden in the damp greyness was revealed when a large house suddenly loomed out of the fog. Somebody shouted a warning over the inter-com but the

Liberator touched the building's roof before taking the tops off a line of nearby trees. The house, known as Plas Heulog, was a substantial residence located on the outskirts of Llanfairfechan. Beyond this building there was little except open hillside, whose contours were completely concealed on that dreary, fog-ridden afternoon.

While the owner of Plas Heulog could count himself fortunate in the extreme — his house had been within a hairsbreadth of being severely damaged or even partly demolished — the same could not be said of the B-24's crew, now fully aware of their plight. A blur of muted green flashed beneath the aircraft, indicating how close the ground was, as Schultz opened the throttles in a last minute bid to gain height. At the same time, a wild, agitated howling, pitiful to hear, emanated from Booster, the crew's pet dog. Human feelings of alarm and fear aroused by the crisis on board had communicated themselves to the unhappy animal, whose canine cries seemed to indicate an awareness that death was imminent. The dog's prescience was soon proved to be correct.

Though the four Pratt and Whitney radial engines, each developing 1,200 h.p., were at maximum power, the effort was to no avail. Barely a mile after skimming Plas Heulog, the aircraft hit the ground with a glancing blow at a small, rocky ridge on the hillside. This collision, according to the official report, damaged and put out of action the no.4, starboard outer engine, though Schultz maintains that it was the no.2, port inner engine that was hit. In addition, the bomb-doors were torn off, leaving spares, luggage and the all-important luxury goods strewn in confusion on the ground as the B-24 lurched violently into the air once again. On the flight deck, pilot and co-pilot were thrown forward with great force against the controls and instrument panel. Unfortunately, Art Davis was not wearing his seat harness and as a result he sustained injuries from which he later died.

Davis' body was draped over the right hand control wheel which, because it was interlocked with the pilots', prevented Schultz from regaining control but after pulling the unconscious co-pilot back into his seat he found that he was able, in a limited way, to fly the aircraft.

By this time, at least two other persons besides P.C. Hughes-Parry had witnessed the B-24's passage overhead; Mr

Robert Jones, who was standing in the grounds of Plas Heulog and Ellis Lewis, a 21 year old farm worker leading a pair of horses along a track which ran through the upland farm of Blaen Llwyn, half a mile from Plas Heulog. Lewis' charges were pulling a cart loaded with stones from a quarry at the nearby village of Penmaenmawr, and as the team approached Blaen Llwyn the aircraft flew past, the thunderous roar of its engines nearly causing the horses to panic. The farm worker was later to play a major part in the rescue operation.

If the official report is correct, then *Bachelors' Baby* first hit the ground at a point 1,200 feet high and immediately to the east of Llanfairfechan but, as with the damage to the engines, Schultz does not agree with this view. He maintains that the bomber was at a much higher altitude, close to 3,000 feet, and some three to four miles further south at the moment of initial impact.

According to his version of events, after contact with the ground the port wing was down and the no. 2 engine was, to use his words, 'All busted up', with pieces of the cowling and nacelle falling away into the slipstream. Two of the propeller blades had gone, while the third was bent backwards. In the cockpit, the rapidly unwinding altimeter indicated a height of 2,800 feet, with the rate of descent shown to be 500 feet a minute. The Artificial Horizon had tumbled but using the Turn and Slip Indicator Schultz was able to bring the wings level. Maintaining or gaining height was impossible though the rate of descent was reduced to 300 feet per minute. Power was increased on no.3 and no.4 engines and full boost given to no.1 engine to compensate for the loss of the second power plant on the port side. Then Schultz applied some right bank and started a shallow turn to starboard, all the while keeping the left wing high. The cloud was so dense that he could barely see the wingtips of his crippled machine.

He remembers the altimeter showing a height of 2,200 feet whereupon he opened the throttles fully but this action failed to halt the aircraft's downward slide. By the time the B-24 was at 1,800 feet Schultz noted the rate of descent had slowed to 100 feet per minute. He tried to gain altitude but the inexorable descent continued until, with the altimeter reading 1,600 feet, a second impact occurred, the actual point being at the foot of a small hill known as Moelfre, three miles to the east of Llanfairfechan.

This time there was a finality about the crash as Schultz once more found himself crushed against the instrument panel, his face in contact with the windscreen as he watched, in what seemed to him to be slow motion, the nose of *Bachelors' Baby* grinding its way with a deafening roar through mud and rocks. Eventually the noise of the aircraft's break up stopped, to be replaced by a short, almost uncanny silence which soon gave way to the hiss and crack of erupting flames as the wreckage caught fire. The bomber's brief career was at an end.

While the precise location of this second impact is established beyond question by physical evidence which remains to this day, there is, as already noted, disagreement as to where the Liberator first made contact with the ground. If we are to believe the official account, then *Bachelor's Baby* collided with a 1,200 feet high ridge ½ a mile to the north west of Moelfre but if Schultz is correct, and as he maintains, the bomber hit at a height close to 3,000 feet, then the point of impact must have been several miles to the south because there are no mountains of this height until the Carneddau are reached.

Is it possible, therefore, given that the pilots' is a dissenting voice, to reconstruct with an accuracy sufficient to eliminate all doubt, the exact flight path of the B-24 during its final moments? We have to concede that the answer is no. As anyone who has investigated a serious accident of any kind will acknowledge, it is not easy to piece together a sequence of events based on the stories of those involved — whether survivors or witnesses — which is entirely free of discrepancy and contradiction, however small. Though this may be frustrating for the investigator or researcher, he or she has to accept that it merely reflects the widely differing levels of perception found among individuals and the fallibility of memory, furthermore.

In the case of *Bachelors' Baby*, the two conflicting accounts cannot satisfactorily be reconciled. Both cannot be correct, so it follows that one must be incorrect — but which one? Schultz asserts that after he started his climbing turn near Bangor he must have flown a course that took him towards Bethesda, to the east of which there are peaks rising to heights of between 1,800 feet and 3,000 feet and into which he drifted during the climb because of the westerly wind blowing that day. To support this claim he cites a number of points: his clear memory of descending with a disabled no.2 engine; the indication given in the accident report that the no.4 propeller and fuselage struck the ground simultaneously, which would not have happened if the B-24 had hit in a climbing left turn; the detail and vividness with which he recalls the instrument readings; the fact that a stone wall at the location quoted in the official report was undamaged, (according to Schultz's calculations the Liberator would have smashed into this wall) and finally, the fact that tail gunner Sergeant Alexander was in his turret when the crash happened. To Schultz this was significant: 'Turret positions were just not manned until a healthy altitude was achieved. I just can't picture Alexander getting into his turret before we had cleared at least a 1,000 feet, certainly not in the weather that we were flying in.'

Against these arguments, which, because they are put forward by the man at the very centre of the disaster, cannot be dismissed out of hand, we have to balance other factors. There was the evidence of the wreckage trail, for instance, and the three witnesses, P.C. Hughes-Parry, Robert Jones and Ellis Lewis, whose testimony, if it did nothing else, proved beyond doubt that *Bachelors' Baby* had flown low over Llanfairfechan.

Confronted by these counter-arguments, though by no means wholly persuaded, Schultz concedes that: 'P.C. Bill Parry's sighting of us flying overhead and the direction of travel after impact seems to indicate that I came busting straight over from the coast and ploughed into the hillside. I suppose it's possible that the instruments could all have been knocked out of whack on that first impact and my memory of fighting the ship down . . . well, I guess it could possibly have occurred in that 800 yard bounce, but somehow I just can't believe it.' We are forced to admit that the fog which obscured Schultz's vision on that day still veils the truth from us.

Let us now return to the much firmer ground of the immediate post-crash scene and subsequent events. After the Liberator's final, terrifying slide, Schultz was in a dazed and injured condition, though luckily his wounds were not excessive or serious; some lacerations and bruising, especially of the left side of his body. He was, however, in a state of deep shock.

As for the cockpit, it had been reduced to a complete wreck.

Much of the floor, extending from the port side to the control pedestal was missing, the armour plating behind the pilot's seat was twisted and there were huge splits in the fuselage on both sides of the flight deck. Schultz himself was wedged between his seat and what remained of the left side of the instrument panel — a position from which he could only free himself by a considerable amount of wriggling, made all the more difficult because of the pain he was experiencing.

In spite of his confused and shocked state of mind, he nevertheless remained alert enough to help the other crew members. 'My whole left side was useless,' he recollects, 'but I took hold of the co-pilot's collar and was trying to lift him on to my right shoulder but I just could not raise him.' Lieutenant Ertz, the Liberator's navigator, himself suffering from spinal injuries, helped to remove the unconscious co-pilot from his seat.

Schultz then went to the assistance of Sergeant Offutt, the flight engineer, who had been trapped in burning wreckage that was rapidly turning into an inferno. The aircraft's top turret had collapsed and pinned the unfortunate man's legs to the floor. Flames were spreading from the bomb-bay (where an extra fuel tank had been fitted) towards the rear part of the turret, threatening to engulf the flight engineer as Schultz went to help him. Offutt's clothes were already smouldering when the pilot made a valiant attempt at rescue. 'I tried to lift the ring of the turret but I couldn't budge it, and it was too hot to handle. It burnt through my gloves. I moved aft for another grip and a large puff of flame blew forward from the bomb-bay, setting alight the right leg of my flying suit. As I bent down to beat out the flames, there was an explosion, (probably caused by the rupturing of the fuel tank). I didn't hear it, I just felt a big whoosh of compression.' Whether he was blown out of the B-24 by this explosion or forced to withdraw because of the intense heat he cannot remember, but the result was the same; sadly, he could make no further attempts at rescuing Offutt, who by then was screaming at Schultz to shoot him before the fire could do its ghastly work. It was a moment of unspeakable horror. Shortly afterwards, the flight engineer succumbed to the flames.

Schultz's next memory is of lying on the ground thirty yards away from the Liberator. Near to the spot where he lay, one of the engines had come to rest after being torn out of its mounting by impact forces. Behind this engine another survivor — 2nd Lt. Jules Ertz — had taken refuge from the fierce heat and exploding ammunition. There, for the time being, the injured pair remained, weakened and inert, as *Bachelors' Baby* turned into a seething cauldron of fire.

Besides Sammy Offutt, two others also perished in the blaze: crewmember Bill Nichols and the passenger Sergeant Cennemo, but in spite of the ferocity of the conflagration, three men were lucky enough to escape with relatively minor injuries: Sergeant Tymczak, Sergeant Neiglos and Lieutenant Boyer, the B-24's bomb-aimer. In the initial confusion of the accident, Boyer assumed that he was the sole survivor until he heard the voices of Schultz and Ertz. Then, above the noise of ammunition rounds detonating in the heat, he could plainly hear shouts for help. Urgently investigating the wreckage he found the rear gunner, Sergeant Alexander, trapped in his turret. Although stunned by the crash, Alexander had quickly regained his senses, only to discover that the turret door was immovably jammed, thus blocking his means of escape.

Knowing that every second counted if he was to avoid the terrible fate of being incinerated alive in the glass and metal cage which the turret had become, he grabbed the crowbar available in his compartment for just such an emergency and began to attack the armoured glass canopy that surrounded him and his guns. With the superhuman strength of a man who is in imminent danger of losing his life, he managed to prise open a section of the glass capsule sufficiently large, or so he thought, to allow an exit. Entering the aperture head first, he began to squeeze out, but to his consternation he could not get his midriff through the gap. Despite twisting and turning in every way possible, he became stuck. To add to his difficulties, the plate of glass he had succeeded in pushing upwards fell back on him, with the result that he was now trapped for the second time.

It was in this position, hanging upside down, half out of the turret, with his head a few feet from the ground that Boyer found him. The bomb-aimer was able to free his ensnared colleague, who in the process fell to the ground and broke his jaw — a small price to pay for deliverance from the rapidly encroaching fire. Boyer then turned his attention to the wrecked main body of the Liberator, where he saw Sergeant Lorenz lying with his legs in the flames. He too was saved from further injury by Boyer.

Meanwhile, external help was approaching. Ellis Lewis, who it will be remembered, was leading a pair of horses along a mountain track near the farm of Blaen Llwyn, had heard the sound of the doomed aircraft's crash. Lewis ran the short distance to the farmhouse and told the farmer, a Mr M.H. Jones, what had happened. The two then hurried to the crash site, easily located in the thick mist because of the fire's orange glow and the sharp, penetrating crack of explosions from burning ammunition. The accident had happened 1½ miles from Blaen Llwyn. Prevented by heat from making a close inspection of the wreckage, the two men searched as best they could and after a brief interval came across Sergeant Alexander lying on the ground, obviously in need of medical attention. The farm labourer decided that the best, indeed the only way to evacuate the airman to safety was to place him on his (Lewis') back and carry him down to Blaen Llwyn. Alexander proved to be a heavy burden during the 1½ mile journey but Lewis was young and strong. From the farmhouse he went to telephone the police and then returned to the quarry at Penmaenmawr, which he had left only a short while previously, there to seek assistance from the workmen, who organised a rescue party without further ado.

Next to arrive at the scene was P.C. Hughes-Parry, breathless and perspiring from the exertion of his climb. He found 2nd Lieutenant Ertz lying alongside the detached engine, unable to walk because of his back injury. Schultz was a few yards away, clearly in a state of confusion. The policeman attempted to assist him by getting hold of his left arm but the pain was too much for Schultz, who struggled to free himself from the well-meaning but unendurable grip of his helper. Hughes-Parry then indicated to him that he should sit on a nearby rock, which he did, while a cigarette was lit and placed between his lips. After surveying the wreckage, the policeman returned to Schultz, removed the cigarette, which was burning the pilot's lips and signalled to him that he was to follow his rescuer downwards. Eventually they reached Llanfairfechan, where a doctor treated the airman's wounds.

Back at the crash site a group of workers from the Penmaenmawr quarry, equipped with stretchers and blankets, were in the process of rescuing five of the crew, all of whom were suffering from injury or shock in varying degrees: Ertz had injured his spine, Neiglos and Tymczak were badly shocked, Art Davis, the co-pilot, had serious head wounds and Bill Lorenz was the victim of extensive burns. The quarrymen carried all five to Blaen Llwyn farm, from where they were taken, together with Schultz, to the C. & A. Hospital in Bangor. It is sad to record that Art Davis and Bill Lorenz later died. The crew's pet dog, Booster, also died in the crash and was buried by Ellis Lewis close to the wreckage.

To complete the narrative of that afternoon's tragic events, it is necessary to turn our attention, once more, to 2nd Lieutenant Boyer. After dragging his two friends, Sergeants Alexander and Lorenz, from the blazing wreckage, Boyer decided to go for help, but in the thick mist which reduced his vision to an almost myopic level, he chose the wrong direction entirely. Instead of going northwards or to the north west, where he would have found habitation — and succour — far sooner than he actually did so, he began to walk in a southerly direction across an area of marsh and bog which, though he could not have known it, only led to higher terrain beyond. Of course, there was no need to seek aid at all — Ellis Lewis and P.C. Hughes-Parry were already on their way, but again the wrecked Liberator's bomb-aimer could not possibly have known this. He reacted, as any man would, instinctively and out of concern for his colleagues.

Struggling to traverse over rough, wet ground and hampered by a painful leg which became increasingly bothersome as time passed, Boyer continued onwards with grim determination, unaware that his journey into unknown territory was unnecessary. To add to his troubles, the mountain mist reduced visibility to no more than a few yards and played its usual trick of distorting perspective and the shape of objects, turning innocuous knolls and boulders into seemingly huge looming giants which threatened to impede his progress. The biggest obstacle, however, was the long ridge of 2,000 feet high Tal-y-Fan mountain, totally hidden by mist but which Boyer successfully negotiated by means of a small dip on its western side, which in the circumstances, he was lucky to find.

From then on he began to descend until he eventually came to an isolated cottage. Its door was locked, so, thoroughly chilled by the dank, clammy mist, he broke in and proceeded to light a fire, in front of which he then warmed himself and attempted to dry some of his wet clothing. Moving on, and downwards, he next came to a farmhouse close to the hamlet of Ro-wen, on the western side of the Conwy valley. Here Boyer, who had walked more than four miles over some very rough ground, was looked after by the farmer and his wife before being taken to a hospital in Llandudno.

By then, US Air Force personnel from RAF Valley had arrived at the crash site and mounted guard over the wreckage. One of Blaen Llwyn's outbuildings was turned into a makeshift operations centre for the guards, salvage men (who removed the wreckage in record time) and accident investigation officers. Some items of food taken from the crashed B-24 were shared with the farmer and Ellis Lewis, who recollects with pleasure the highly appreciated munificence of the Americans in giving him: 'Tins and tins of peaches and cigarettes galore!' He eventually took over the farm of Blaen Llwyn and has remained there to this day, his vigour and sense of humour undiminished by the passing years.

As Lewis had been responsible for carrying Sergeant Alexander down the mountainside, the airman wanted to reward his rescuer, as did the other crew members, particularly for burying Booster, for whom they clearly had much affection. Unable to contact the farm worker because the survivors were not informed where they had crashed, Alexander overcame this difficulty by bribing one of the nurses at the hospital into providing him with the necessary address. As a result, Lewis, to his complete surprise, found himself presented with a £5 note — a substantial sum of money in 1944. He had hardly seen a note of this denomination previously and was most touched by the men's generous offering.

Within a few days of the crash, all of the bomber's crew were transferred to US military hospitals in the United Kingdom, where they continued their recovery. Some regained their health quickly, others did not, especially Schultz, who spent a lengthy period of hospitalisation and convalescence, first in Britain and then the United States. So deep was the trauma inflicted on his psyche by the accident that for several weeks afterwards he remained confused, disorientated and had considerable difficulty in coherent speech. Furthermore, he suffered a partial loss of memory which wiped out much of his recollection of the tragedy, yet left some scenes, stark and vivid in their detail, indelibly etched on his mind.

Gradually, over the following months the extent of Schultz's amnesia receded as his general condition improved. In time, his memory of that fateful day was restored, though only partly and some crucial gaps remained, like missing pieces of a jigsaw puzzle. His inability to fill those gaps was, as he admits, a particular source of worry and irritation to him. On countless occasions he would force himself to go over the nightmarish details of the crash but was never able to resolve his dilemma; whether the story, as he remembered it, was factually complete or not. Scenes of the Liberator's last moments, whenever he conjured them up in his mind always had a searing sense of reality inextricably interwoven with a dream-like state, or even hallucination, thus perpetually thwarting the man's desire to establish the veracity of his recollections.

Every time he lowered a bucket into the well of his memory, so to speak, the pure water of truth that he wanted seemed to be contaminated by delusion and falsehood. Despite endless pondering on the subject, doubt and uncertainty continued to haunt him and were to do so for many years. Three decades, no less, were to pass before the final pieces of the jigsaw fell into place.

In August 1944, eight months after the loss of *Bachelors' Baby*, Schultz's period of recuperation was over, as were his flying days, officially at least. Denied a medical category by the military authorities that would allow him to continue as a pilot, he had to relinquish aircrew status without ever having dropped a single bomb on the enemy. He remained in the Air Force, however, where he held a number of administrative posts both home and abroad, until his retirement in October 1962, by which time he had attained the rank of Major.

But that is not quite the end of the story; there is a sequel, which to some extent parallels that described in chapter 5 and which took place more than thirty years after the time of the accident. Among Llanfairfechan's residents in the 1970s was a retired civil servant by the name of Jack Bohanna, for whom the tale of *Bachelors' Baby* had been one of intense fascination since he first came to know of the aircraft and its tragic fate. So strong was the hold the Liberator had on his mind that he decided to trace the surviving crew members. Bohanna knew full well that this was a far from easy task, with failure just as much of a possibility as success, but the challenge was a stimulating one for him and furthermore, because of his abiding interest in the crash he was a keen and highly motivated researcher. In a spirit of optimism he set about his quest early in 1976, hoping that he would succeed in contacting some, if not all, of the crew. The achievement of his objective, as he had anticipated, was not immediate by any means; writing numerous letters produced either no response from recipients or the cul-de-sac of a negative reply. Nevertheless, Bohanna remained indefatigable. Then, in November 1977 his singleminded, unremitting efforts were finally rewarded when, through the co-operation of the International Liberator Club, he managed to track down Ace Schultz, who, it turned out, was living in Palmetto, Florida.

A correspondence ensued between the two, and in 1978, through the exhortations of his new friend, Schultz returned to Llanfairfechan and the crash site. When he set foot once again on the patch of ground where he had last stood in January 1944, many long repressed memories and seemingly forgotten details of the accident came back to him. After a gap of thirty years and more, the recollections of that January day were as fully restored as they ever could be to Schultz. Having arrived in Llanfairfechan still troubled by past events, he departed a freer, less burdened man. Shafts of light had been thrown into the dark shadows of the past and no longer would the ghost of *Bachelors' Baby* haunt him.

For this welcome relief he owed a considerable debt of gratitude to Jack Bohanna, whose original initiative in the mid 1970s and subsequent researches into the story of the crashed Liberator were to prove so beneficial not only to Schultz in particular but also to aviation historians in general. Schultz's visit to North Wales in 1978 was to become the first of several in the years that followed.

As the friendship between the American ex-pilot and Bohanna grew ever-more cordial, the latter, who had already placed a small wooden cross at the crash site in November 1975, expressed a desire to replace the cross with a more fitting, permanent memorial to those crew members who had died. This memorial was to be in the form of a slate plaque, paid for by Bohanna and a number of like-minded colleagues.

Thus on the morning of 20th March 1980, with a cold wind blowing, and a blanket of snow on the ground, an US Air Force helicopter airlifted a group of twenty men to the bleak, desolate hillside of Moelfre. The principal members of the assembly were Ace Schultz, ex-P.C. Hughes-Parry, Ellis Lewis, and the Reverend J. Elwyn Jones, rector of Llanfairfechan, while the remainder of the party was comprised mostly of local aviation enthusiasts, plus a sprinkling of newspaper and television reporters. But there was one individual missing from the group, and whose absence was regretted by everyone; Jack Bohanna, the person whose detective work was primarily responsible for bringing about that morning's proceedings. To his profound disappointment he had been forced by the inclement weather to abandon the trip and had to be content with watching the helicopter's departure from Llanfairfechan.

After a short religious ceremony, the slate plaque, mounted on a rock cairn, was unveiled by Schultz, who commented on the kindness of those who had rendered assistance to him: 'You are the most warm-hearted people that I have ever met, you will always be my dearest friends and I thank you very much.'

Another survivor from the crew of *Bachelors' Baby* — Jules Ertz — was also contacted, and he too returned to Llanfairfechan, in 1984. After his war service he became a lawyer, practising in Los Angeles. Since the accident he has always suffered from back pain arising out of the spinal injuries he received.

In 1990 Jack Bohanna died and his ashes were scattered on the crash site of *Bachelors' Baby* as were his wife's when she died in 1993, just before Ace Schultz and his wife, Lois, were due to visit her. The American couple did, however, join members of the Bohanna family on the mountainside in order to assist in the final duty of scattering Mrs Bohanna's ashes.

A visitor to Moelfre hill today would find no trace of wreckage, all of which was removed immediately after the crash. Only the memorial plaque remains to mark the spot where the Liberator and five of its crew met their untimely end. Curiously enough, the actual piece of ground, the few square yards where the aircraft finally came to rest and caught fire are clearly delineated from the surrounding area by a total lack of vegetation cover. Not a single blade of grass has grown here since 1944; there is nothing but bare soil and a few stones. It seems that the fierce heat of the post-crash fire released chemicals and toxins of some kind into the ground, which in consequence, has become completely barren.

Chapter 8

In the Dark

The year of 1944 had started badly for the American unit at RAF Valley with the loss of B-24 *Bachelors' Baby* early in January, and though no other major accidents occurred, with the exception of a Dakota crash, the year was destined to end on a tragic note when an inbound Liberator was lost after crashing into the sea off Holyhead a few days before Christmas.

The Dakota in question came to grief on 2 September when attempting to land with its starboard engine on fire. On final approach and shortly before touchdown, the burning engine became detached from its mounting in the wing and fell to the ground, landing with a mighty thud fifty yards from Rhosneigr Golf Club, leaving the occupants of the clubhouse to ponder upon their narrow escape! The Dakota's pilot, meanwhile, managed to land safely, despite having to cope with a wing on fire and with one engine physically missing from his machine. All the crew escaped without injury, leaving the aircraft to be destroyed by fire.

Much more serious, however, was the loss of a Liberator three months later, in December. The aircraft, serial number 42-51232 and named *The Jig's Up*, was one of a flight of seven B-24s from the air base at Cheddington who had been operating a radio jamming mission in Europe, but on their return bad weather had forced a diversion from their home station to RAF Manston, in Kent. On 22 December the flight became airborne at 1.30 p.m. with the intention of flying back to their base. Each aircraft had 1,000 gallons of fuel on board because the weather at Cheddington was marginal and further diversions might be necessary. Flying Control at the station made arrangements, at 1.45 p.m., for a possible diversion to Valley, where the weather was equally as marginal as at Cheddington; 7/10s cloud at an average of 1,200 feet, overcast at 2,000 feet and visibility down to one mile — a typically murky winter afternoon, in fact.

When the B-24s arrived at Cheddington, conditions there were so bad the airfield had been forced to close, as a result of which the flight was then diverted to RAF Atcham, near Shrewsbury, arriving there at 4.00 p.m. Four out of the seven aircraft managed to get through the low cloud and land successfully, but the remaining three were unable to do so; they had to fly in circles, waiting for either a sudden break in the clouds or an alternative plan to be put into action. A few minutes before 5.00 p.m. RAF Valley was advised by Atcham that the three aircraft, including *The Jig's Up* (whose radio callsign was 'Marker Jig'), were being diverted to Anglesey. They were expected to arrive at 5.30 p.m. By the time this message was received, darkness had fallen, and so had the cloudbase at Valley, where it was now down to 500 feet.

Shortly after 5.15 p.m. 'Marker Jig' arrived in the local area. The pilot informed Valley that he was 'On top [of the cloud layer] at 4,000 feet with two and one half hours fuel on board.' Unfortunately, however, the latter half of the message was wildly inaccurate because the pilot had badly misjudged how much fuel remained. The reality was that the Liberator's tanks were almost empty: 'Marker Jig' could stay airborne for only another fifteen minutes or so, though all concerned with the safety of the aircraft remained blissfully unaware of this fact.

Valley's control tower then asked if the B-24 could complete a procedure let-down on the radio range (an early form of assisted landing system) to which the pilot replied that he had no relevant local information and that his 'Gee' navigational aid system had become inoperative at Atcham. He was told to standby as there were other aircraft letting down at that time. For the next few minutes 'Marker Jig' did nothing except maintain its position, as the pilot, little knowing that an emergency was imminent, probably wondered how and when he was going to reach the safety of the runway somewhere below in the winter darkness. He never did reach that runway because shortly after 5.30 p.m. time ran out for the B-24. As the fuel tanks became dry, first, one engine stopped, then a few moments later a second, closely followed by a third.

Once he had informed Valley of the situation, the pilot ordered his crew of eight men to bale out. The aircraft's precise location at that moment is not known but it is clear, from subsequent events, that it was at some point to the western, seaward side of the airfield.

At 5.40 p.m. a coastguard on duty at Gogarth Bay, the area of forbiddingly steep cliffs between the North and South Stacks, immediately to the west of Holyhead Mountain, observed a vivid flash close to the North Stack. Moments later, the flash was followed by the sounds of an explosion which signalled the destruction of the Liberator as it dashed itself to smithereens against the precipitous rocks of Gogarth. The coastguard hurriedly contacted his headquarters at Holyhead and an extensive search was set in motion at once, using every available man but after two hours of intense, concentrated activity only two of the B-24's occupants were found floating in the water; the pilot, rescued near Holyhead and the co-pilot, picked up at Trearddur Bay. Of the others there was no sign. After questioning the survivors it became evident that their colleagues had parachuted from the aircraft when it was over the sea and because none of the eight wore a life-jacket they drowned.

At the inquiry which followed, a number of criticisms were voiced by the Investigating Committee, whose members were all senior American Air Force officers. They blamed Cheddington's flying control section for failing to divert the seven B-24s immediately to Valley after it was realised that they could not land at their home base. Much valuable time had been lost by sending the flight to Atcham, where the weather was poor. The unfortunate pilot of 'Marker Jig' also received criticism for failing to keep an accurate check on the fuel consumption of his aircraft. He admitted that when the engines stopped he had not been aware of the dangerously low fuel state. Giving evidence to the Committee, he readily conceded that the only plausible cause for the almost simultaneous failure of all the engines was lack of petrol. The inquiry could not have been anything except a painfully grim ordeal for him; besides having to bear the burden of losing most of his crew, he was now being officially censured for his mistakes.

A further contributary cause of the accident, in the Committee's view, was the fact that the crew had not been properly briefed on the local terrain and airfield facilities. They were depending entirely on the B-24's 'G-Box' for navigation and when this device broke down, the crew had no means of making an exact check on their position. Furthermore, the hapless pilot had no knowledge whatsoever of the radio range at Valley, and neither did he know the position of the mountains in relation to the airfield. Worse still was the fact that at the time he gave the order to bale out, he did not know Valley was situated on the coast of an island and therefore there was a strong possibility, if not a certainty, that his fellow crew members would end up in the sea, which of course they did. When those men jumped out of their doomed aircraft on that winter's evening they were metaphorically as well as literally in the dark.

Robert Loraine's biplane at Llanfairynghornwy in 1910
(photo: Gwynedd Archives)

Loraine (seated) looks on while his mechanic, Jules Vedrines,
carries out adjustments
(photo: RAF Museum)

*A Hawker Audax similar to the two which crashed near RAF Penrhos
in November 1937
(photo: MAP)*

*The tangled wreckage of Anson K6227 lies on Penmaenmawr beach
(photo: via Elfyn Williams)*

An aerial view of RAF Penrhos in 1938
(photo: via O. Roberts)

A de Havilland Puss Moth similar to the one which crashed at Broom Hall
in April 1937
(photo: MAP)

A Blackburn Skua similar to the one which crashed on Elidir Fawr in 1941
(photo: IWM)

Flight Lieutenant Graham,
originator of the RAF's Mountain Rescue organisation
(photo: via A. Evans)

A Bristol Beaufighter of 456 Squadron and sister aircraft of the Beaufighter which crashed at Newborough Warren
(photo: via Jack Ross)

Remains of the 'Q' Site at Newborough Warren photographed in 1990. The site was subsequently buried under tons of sand
(photo: Roy Sloan)

Kurt Schlender (left) and Lothar Horras (right) meet on the slopes of Llwytmor in August 1989
(photo: HTV)

Lothar Horras at the controls of a Heinkel bomber. Behind Horras is the Flight Engineer Josef Brüninghausen, who was killed in the Llwytmor crash
(photo: HTV)

Llandwrog airfield photographed from the air in 1987
(photo: Roy Sloan)

An Armstrong Whitworth Whitley similar to the pair that collided in mid-air
over RAF Llandwrog in October 1941
(photo: IWM)

The crew of "Bachelors' Baby": front row, left to right — Sammy Offutt,
John Tymczak, Joe Neiglos, Bill Lorenz, Bill Nichols
and Harold Alexander.
Back row, left to right — Ace Schultz, Art Davis, Norman Boyer, Jules Ertz
(photo: via A. Evans)

A B-24 Liberator similar to "Bachelors' Baby", which crashed on
high ground above Llanfairfechan in January 1944. The aircraft
illustrated is about to land at RAF Valley
(photo: USAAF)

Memorial service held at the crash site of "Bachelors' Baby". From left to right: Elwyn Ellis, Ellis Lewis, Jack Bohanna, ?, the Rev. J. Elwyn Jones (photo: via Mrs Y. Elwyn Jones)

Crash site of "Bachelors' Baby", with the slate memorial and wooden cross seen on the right (photo: Roy Sloan)

*The Anglesey lane where Dr Chill and his family met their deaths
in the crash of Wellington DV455, 19 July 1943
(photo: Roy Sloan)*

*A slate memorial tablet located close to the crash site of Dakota EI-AFL
in Cwm Edno. The inscription reads: 'On the night of 10 January 1952
close to this vicinity a C-47 Dakota EI-AFL, the St. Kevin, crashed.
All on board perished. R.I.P.
(photo: Roy Sloan)*

*An Aer Lingus Dakota and sister-ship of the one that crashed
in Cwm Edno in January 1952
(photo: A. P. Publications)*

*The remains of Dakota EI-AFL lie in a Snowdonia bog. Shortly after the
photograph was taken (1980) all traces of wreckage were removed
(photo: Roy Sloan)*

The Snowdon Mountain Railway on the upper slopes of the mountain.
A train is at the spot where Anson VM407 crashed
(photo: Roy Sloan)

The wreckage of Vulcan XA909 lies burning in a field near Gwalchmai
on 16 July 1964
(photo: via Hugh Williams)

*View from the landing pad at Rhosgoch oil farm from which helicopter
G-BBIU took off on 25 October 1979 and crashed into power lines
only 200 yards away
(photo: Roy Sloan)*

*A Hughes 269C helicopter similar to the ones that crashed at
Rhosgoch and Betws-y-coed in 1979
(photo: MAP)*

*The rocky outcrop of Clogwyn-y-Cyrau above Betws-y-coed,
where helicopter G-CHIC crashed in November 1979
(photo: Roy Sloan)*

*A Hawker Siddeley Gnat trainer of No.4 FTS, RAF Valley
and sister aircraft of Gnat XR 950 which crashed at Carmel
in April 1965 following a mid-air collision
(photo: MAP)*

A Hawker Hunter T.7 similar to the one that crashed
in Cwm Penmachno in May 1971
(photo: MAP)

Cwm Penmachno on a stormy day in September 1991.
A ray of sunshine breaks through the clouds to illuminate the area
where Hunter T.7 XL622 crashed in May 1971
(photo: Roy Sloan)

Piper Cherokee 140 G-AVWG being dismantled after a forced landing on Tal-y-Fan mountain in December 1988
(photo: Roy Sloan)

A Piper Twin Comanche similar to the one which crashed on Crib-y-Ddysgl in October 1972
(photo: MAP)

Chapter 9

A Million To One Chance

Tucked away in an inside page of the *North Wales Chronicle* for 22 August 1941 was the following item of news:

'**A Doctor & His Petrol Coupon**; For the alleged unlawful use of a supplementary petrol coupon exchanged at Cambridge on June 19th, Mark William Chill, medical practitioner of Trygarn, Bodedern was, at Cambridge, on Friday, fined £5. He was asked why he had used this coupon and in a letter said he had used his basic ration for his practice and not for private purposes and, as he had been considerably overworked, owing to the wideness of his practice, he went for a short holiday at Cambridge. He admitted going to see the Derby and the Oaks.'

Misuse of strictly rationed petrol during wartime there may have been, so that the doctor could enjoy some horse-racing but few of his patients would have reproached him for his misdemeanour. Forgiveness would be easy for most, because Dr Chill was a popular man, held in great esteem in the Anglesey village of Bodedern, from where he ran his large rural practice. What he could not have known at the time, however, was that petrol would be the substance responsible for causing his death, and that of his wife and mother-in-law some two years later, in an aircraft accident.

Dr Chill came to Bodedern in the summer of 1939 when he was 60 years old and quickly established himself as an efficient and caring GP who ministered to the needs of the sick with tireless energy. Bespectacled and invariably dressed in a brown suit and with a trilby hat on his head, the doctor could be abrupt and forthright in his manner, overbearing even, at times — a characteristic, some said, which arose from his background. He had gone out to the Far East, to practise medicine in the British colony of the Straits Settlements on the Malay peninsula and there he became used to the habit, not unknown amongst colonial Englishmen, of treating the indigenous population as inferior in strength of character and ability to their British masters; a habit which, apparently, the medic could not quite shake off when working and living in Bodedern.

Chill shared his large, rambling house with his wife, Marjorie, a strikingly attractive young woman less than half her husband's age and only 30 years old when she met her untimely death. She was, in fact, Chill's second wife, as his first marriage had ended in divorce. The other person in the doctor's household was his elderly mother-in-law though it is not recorded if this arrangement added to or subtracted from the total sum of his happiness! He drove a dark blue Morris motor car and when on his rounds, would more often than not, be accompanied by his wife and her mother. The Morris, with its three occupants, was a familiar sight on the roads in and around Bodedern.

Let us now move forward two years from the time of the petrol coupon affair to the summer of 1943; Monday 19 July to be precise. In the morning Chill had held a surgery, then called upon some patients and after lunch he was planning to drive the four miles or so to the nearby village of Llanddeusant in order to visit some more patients before driving another three miles to the next village, Llanrhyddlad, where he would hold an afternoon surgery.

The weather on that Monday was particularly fine, with clear skies and a hot sun radiating its heat over the Anglesey countryside. For the farmers it was an ideal day for haymaking and many were busy in meadows throughout the length and breadth of the island doing just that. In the middle of the afternoon, however, there occurred an alarming diversion for those working in the fields on the north western side of Anglesey. Shortly after 2.30 p.m. the steady drone of an aircraft became audible and anyone looking upwards would have seen a large twin-engined machine flying overhead. But not for long, because the regular beat of the engines suddenly faltered, and the aircraft, a Vickers Wellington bomber, started to fall out of the sky.

Two and a half hours earlier, the Wellington was parked on the apron at the Leicestershire airfield of RAF Castle Donington, the home of No. 28 Operational Training Unit and to whom the aircraft belonged. This machine, (serial number DV455), was to be flown on a training flight during the afternoon by a five man crew and at midday they climbed into the bomber which then taxied out to the runway and after a normal take-off run, became airborne.

The flight would take the crew to North Wales, a region used extensively by Midlands-based RAF OTUs for training purposes and where the five men, with a Canadian pilot, Sergeant F. Chase as skipper, would use the time spent flying in the area learning to work together efficiently as a team. This was an important aspect of their training, as success, and indeed their very survival as individuals, depended more than anything else upon good teamwork, when operational flying with a front-line squadron would become a reality for them. It was vital, therefore, to weld the five into a confident, working group, but this particular flight would contribute little to that goal.

As noted already, just after 2.30 p.m. the Wellington was flying over northern Anglesey when the port engine suddenly lost its unceasing rhythm and then hiccuped a few times before spluttering to a stop. Moments later it caught fire. As all pilots know, any fire in the air, however small, is extremely serious and has to be dealt with immediately, which Sergeant Chase proceeded to do, but no sooner had he turned his attention to the failed port engine than the starboard engine also began to lose power.

Assuming the fire did not spread too rapidly, it might have been possible to maintain height on one engine, if it was nursed gently, long enough to make an emergency landing at RAF Valley, only a few miles distant, but as the second engine came to a stop almost as quickly as the first, then this option could not be considered any further. The situation on board DV455 was rapidly becoming critical. Faced with a total loss of power, Sergeant Chase, now sitting in a strangely silent cockpit, after the reassuring roar of the engines had died away, knew the aircraft had to be abandoned and so he ordered the crew to bale out.

Four men left the doomed bomber, two of whom, Sergeants Greenwood and Wilcox landed uninjured while the third, Sergeant Gwardney, the bomb aimer, was slightly injured. Unfortunately, the parachute harness of the fourth man, Sergeant R. Jepson, the wireless operator, was not properly fastened and became detached when he jumped. He fell to earth and was killed instantly.

In the aircraft, Sergeant Chase, once his crew had gone, prepared to jump. His final act, before doing so, was to point the machine's nose seawards. As the northern coastline of Anglesey was close, a crash into the sea would eliminate the possibility of causing injury or death to those on the ground, or damage to their property. 'I trimmed the aircraft to fly into the sea,' said Chase, 'and prayed to God that it would do so.' It did not, however. Perversely it seemed, once free of human control, the Wellington swung round and headed inland, leaving its pilot to float down by parachute towards the green patchwork of fields below. He landed without injury.

Meanwhile, DV455 continued on its capricious path, losing height all the time and at a rate which indicated that its end would not be long delayed. The final plunge, when it came, was 1½ miles to the north of Bodedern, in a field of oats. Watched from the next field by two terrified farm workers, who had dived for cover underneath their haycart, the bomber slid along the ground until it hit a bank of earth which separated one side of the oatfield from an adjoining lane. Momentum carried the now disintegrating aircraft forward with such force that it punched a huge hole in this obstruction, sending a shower of burning wreckage into the lane and a field beyond. The time was 2.45 p.m.

We must now return to Dr Chill, who, it will be remembered, was that afternoon intending to drive to Llanddeusant. His route, along which he had travelled so many times before, was a delightful rural byway deep in the Anglesey countryside where, on that day of warm sunshine, a glorious verdancy was displayed from every hedge, wood, grove, and pasture. The doctor was, of course, completely unaware of the Wellington's flight and the engine failure which forced the crew to abandon their craft.

After lunch Chill had said goodbye to his housekeeper and receptionist, Miss Mair Hughes, and set off in his car, accompanied as ever by his wife and mother-in-law but he drove only a few hundred yards from his home when he realised that he had forgotten a bag of instruments. The GP stopped his car and returned to the house, where he picked up the missing bag before setting off once again. He could not have known how dire the consequences of this slight delay would be for himself and his family. A few minutes later, with the time approaching 2.45 p.m., the doctor's Morris crossed the tiny bridge that spans the Alaw, a small river to the north of Bodedern. The car then climbed a brief rise to reach a cluster of buildings; the country church of

Llanfugail, secluded and peaceful, a nearby farm and a large house known as Plas Llanfugail — set in as charming and attractive a spot as one would be likely to find in Anglesey.

Here the road curved slightly to the left and back again, before descending a little and straightening out. On this section, hedgerows on the car's nearside were low and afforded a view of the fields beyond, but the right-hand hedge was significantly taller, with a luxuriant growth of mid-summer foliage screening off the land behind from sight. Where the gentle descent ended, there was an entrance on the left, leading to the farm of Tyddyn Watcyn and it was at the moment when his car was passing this opening that Dr Chill's world came to an end.

Suddenly the air was filled with a tearing, crashing roar and the hedge a few yards in front of the car, on its right-hand side, seemed to dissolve in a huge explosion which scattered earth, stones and pieces of burning aircraft wreckage everywhere. In an instant the Morris was brought to a halt and before any of the car's occupants had time to comprehend the calamity that had so violently overtaken them, flames engulfed the vehicle. A pleasant drive in the country had ended in a ghastly nightmare.

Dr Chill had suffered the greatest misfortune to be at the precise point where Wellington DV455 hit the bank of earth. Only a few seconds before, or after the crash, and he would have most probably escaped with nothing worse than scratched or blistered paintwork on his car. Or if the hedgerow had not been so high, then he might have been able to see the aircraft approach and could have stopped his car in time to prevent any damage. However, it was not to be, and the million to one chance, statistically so remote, of being hit by a crashing aircraft became a grim reality for three very unlucky people.

Though seriously burned, the doctor managed to escape from his blazing car and would have survived if he had not attempted to rescue his wife and mother-in-law. In a desperate effort he succeeded in getting his wife out of the vehicle and he then pushed her into a roadside ditch but extricating his 73 year old mother-in-law from the consuming flames was too much for him. Giving up the struggle to help the older woman, he stumbled weakly towards Plas Llanfugail, some two hundred yards away. The occupant of this house, Mrs Grace Pritchard, had heard the tremendous commotion of the crash and upon rushing outside saw the Wellington's tailplane on fire, close to her home. She then began to run to the main wreckage and was met by Dr Chill coming towards her, with his clothes on fire. In an endeavour to extinguish the flames, Mrs Pritchard took off some of her own clothes and wrapped them around the medic before rolling him on the ground. So bad were the doctor's burns, however, that he had become facially unrecognisable and Grace Pritchard thought that she was assisting a stranger.

But Chills' overriding concern was for his wife, as he exclaimed: 'My wife, my wife. Go and see what you can do for her.' Obediently, Mrs Pritchard went to the wreckage strewn in the road but she could not see anything at all because of the fire and billowing smoke. It was not until later that she discovered there was a car amidst all the aircraft debris.

Others were now hurrying to the scene, including a young naval officer by the name of Ernest Naish, who for the past few days had been enjoying a period of leave, spent at home on his family's farm near Bodedern. Agriculture held an abiding interest for him and he was never more content than when working in the fields, where he happened to be, thinning some turnips, when he saw the Wellington's final dive to the ground. Naish then grabbed a bicycle and started to pedal furiously, going 'like the wind', in his own words, towards the scene of the crash. Before reaching the actual wreckage, however, he came upon an injured man lying in the road. This man, as the reader will have guessed, was Dr Chill, but Naish, like Grace Pritchard previously, did not recognise the GP because of the severity of his facial disfigurement. Assuming him to be one of the Wellington's crew, Naish was somewhat puzzled to note the 'airman' did not have an uniform, as one would expect in the case of RAF aircrew. Instead, the man was wearing civilian clothes and a striped tie. Pushing this thought to the back of his mind, Naish, together with another farmer who had just arrived, began to attend to the man, who then spoke in a gravelly voice: 'What about my wife and mother-in-law? Are they safe?' he asked. Clearly, what remained uppermost in Chill's mind was the welfare of his family.

Ernest Naish recognised the voice instantly and with a realisation that made his blood run cold. The grievously burned person lying on the ground in front of him was no airman or Air Ministry official as he first thought, but none other than his own doctor, a man he knew well and for whom he had the greatest respect. Deeply dismayed and shocked by this discovery, Naish nevertheless kept his wits about him and ran to investigate the fate of the two women. Sadly, both were dead. Marjorie Chill lay in the ditch where her husband had placed her in a vain attempt to save her life, while her mother was still inside the fiercely burning car. Fuel from the crashed Wellington had set the whole area ablaze and neither woman had any chance of survival in this inferno.

Meanwhile, back in the doctor's house, his receptionist and housekeeper, Mair Hughes, was going about her duties when the telephone rang. She lifted the handset to her ear and heard a male voice (she never discovered the caller's identity but he was probably someone from one of the farms close to the crash) telling her in an excited and not very coherent manner about the accident and asking if Dr Chill could go to the scene immediately. Obviously, neither party in this conversation was aware of the truth and Miss Hughes responded simply by saying that her employer had gone to Llanddeusant. Later, when she knew the facts, she reflected how ironic it was that someone should unwittingly ask for the doctor's help at the crash site when Chill and his family were themselves the victims of the accident.

Ernest Naish and a neighbouring farmer had, meantime, taken the doctor by car to the nearest hospital, at Valley, but Chill died there on the following day. The extent and seriousness of his burns, and the circumstances of the tragedy caused great distress to the hospital staff, to many of whom the GP was a friend and colleague. He and his wife were buried a few days later at Bodedern while his mother-in-law's body was taken to London for burial. Undeniably, the three had suffered a terrible fate.

After the war ended, Ernest Naish, who had by then reached the rank of Commander, left the Royal Navy and returned to his other love — farming. Working the land, he said, gave him a sense of deep satisfaction and well-being which he did not find in other occupations. In 1959 he decided to buy a second farm and eventually purchased one in Cwm Pennant, an outstandingly beautiful part of Snowdonia. Here, during the early 1960s he was enjoying the arduous, but for him, immensely rewarding task of managing an upland farm.

One day in 1963 he was sitting at home reading *The Times* when in the course of glancing casually at the newspaper's 'personal' column his eye was caught by a reference to a 'Dr Chill'. The name immediately rekindled the farmer's memories of that painful afternoon in July 1943. 'Could this man be the Chill I knew?' he asked himself. It was.

Eagerly Naish read the item — a request from a woman living in Australia for information about her brother, once a member of the Straits Settlement Medical Service, she said, and whom she believed to have died in an accident somewhere in Britain. From his conversations with the doctor when he was alive, Naish knew Chill had practised medicine in the Far East and that he had relatives living in Australia. There and then the farmer wrote a letter to the woman, explaining in detail what had happened to the doctor. The letter of thanks Naish received in reply confirmed that the woman was indeed Chill's sister. In the way that family members sometimes drift apart and do not maintain any kind of relationship, she had lost touch completely with her brother and wanted to know, for her own peace of mind, if reports of his death had any truth or not. By a remarkable stroke of luck, another million to one chance, one is tempted to say, she had succeeded in making contact with the very man who had assisted her brother as he lay, horribly burned, in that Anglesey lane twenty years previously.

There is one small footnote to add to this story of a chance in a million; on the 24 April 1961 a Vampire T.11 jet trainer from RAF Valley got into a spin from which it failed to recover. The two occupants abandoned the aircraft, leaving it to crash in the same field as the Wellington in 1943.

Chapter 10

The Last Flight of Dakota EI-AFL

Shortly after 5.00 p.m. on Thursday 10 January 1952 twenty passengers boarded an Aer Lingus DC-3 Dakota at Northolt aerodrome, near London. The aircraft was bound for Dublin, that most attractive of cities, but tragically, none of the passengers or crew would reach their journey's end. Instead, they were destined to become the victims of Gwynedd's worst civil aviation disaster, following the airliner's crash in a remote part of Snowdonia.

The Dakota, registered EI-AFL and named *St Kevin*, after the Irish saint, was used frequently by Aer Lingus on their regular run between London and Dublin. This particular machine had been built in 1944 for service with the USAAF, had then been transferred to the RAF and in the post-war years, like so many other ex-military Dakotas, it had found its way into civilian hands. In April 1950 it was purchased by Aer Lingus, to add to their fleet of DC-3s. Commercial operators such as the Irish airline bought surplus Dakotas in large numbers primarily because these machines provided excellent value for money. The type's virtues as an outstandingly reliable military transport during the Second World War also made it a safe, economical airliner in peacetime. In fact, from the beginning of the DC-3's development by the Douglas Corporation in the mid-1930s, company engineers realised they had a first-rate design on their hands, and the type is now universally acknowledged to be one of the most successful aircraft of all time. Even today, DC-3s remain in service throughout the world and will, without a doubt, continue to do so into the next century.

But such considerations hardly entered into the minds of the passengers on board EI-AFL as they waited for take-off on that typically cold and dreary winter evening. All they desired was to reach their destination safely and as soon as possible. At 5.15 p.m. the aircraft rolled down the runway and was quickly drawn skywards by the sureness of two Pratt and Whitney radial engines at full power, their deep, throbbing roar piercing the January gloom as the Dakota headed northwards.

In charge was Captain James Keohane, an experienced pilot with 4,887 flying hours entered in his logbook. He had two crew members; the co-pilot, First Officer Newman, and 23 year old air hostess Deirdre Sutton. Both pilots had flown the London-Dublin route many times before, the previous occasion being that afternoon, when they had made an outward trip from the Irish capital. Now on the return run, the Dakota's track would first take it to Daventry in the Midlands, then to North Wales, where the Nefyn radio beacon provided a suitable point at which to cross the coast before flying over the Irish Sea on the final leg of a journey which was due to end at Dublin Airport.

The duty weather forecaster at Northolt that afternoon was a woman by the name of Joan McKay, who provided Captain Keohane with a report indicating 60 knot westerly winds at 5,000 feet, freezing levels at 8,000 feet, rising towards the end of the flight to 9,000 feet. Icing conditions were described as 'Slight to moderate'. To deal with this hazard, the aircraft was fitted with standard anti-icing and de-icing equipment which met all the airworthiness requirements.

At first, the flight proved uneventful. The Dakota, flying at 4,500 feet, reached Daventry on schedule and was soon approaching the Welsh border, where turbulence was encountered. To escape the worst of this rough air Captain Keohane requested permission from Preston air traffic control centre to climb to 6,500 feet. Permission was granted and the pilot later reported that he was at this height. However, the air remained disturbed, much to the discomfort of the passengers.

Besides the Dakota there were other aircraft aloft in the region and it was to the pilot of one that Captain Keohane spoke: 'You'll find it pretty rough over the hills tonight. We were at 4,500 feet and went up to 6,500 feet and it seems to be rough right through.' This proved to be the only comment on weather conditions made by EI-AFL's crew. Transcriptions of their radio calls revealed no anxiety on their part about bad weather, or navigational problems which might have arisen thereupon.

In contrast, another of Aer Lingus' pilots, Captain Wallace, returning from Paris to Dublin, was most concerned about the stormy conditions over the Welsh hills. He had encountered severe turbulence and icing which became worse as the aircraft flew further westwards. Because of the icing, airspeed had decreased steadily from 130 knots and by the time it was down to an alarming 105 knots, Wallace had had enough and decided to divert to Liverpool, where he made a safe landing. Later, his co-pilot, First Officer Ross Kelly, described the icing as: 'More severe than anything I have experienced before. Turbulence was very bad too, although I have known it as bad on other occasions.'

Meanwhile, Captain Keohane, in his DC-3, was approaching the Nefyn beacon, or so he thought and just after 7.10 p.m. contacted Dublin air traffic control. 'We checked over Nefyn a minute ago,' he informed them, 'flying 6,500 feet under IFR. Request descent clearance.' At 7.14 p.m. Dublin gave the required clearance but could not contact the Dakota to indicate this fact. Despite repeated attempts, no further contact was made. So what had become of the aircraft?

It had, without the crew's knowledge, been blown many miles off course by the strong winds. When Keohane reported passing the Nefyn beacon he was, in fact, badly mistaken. In reality the DC-3 was twenty miles away from this point, flying over Snowdonia and rapidly approaching Snowdon itself. Some two miles south of the mountain lies a beautiful valley, Nant Gwynant, beyond which, and again to the south, there is an upland area composed of minor peaks interspersed with cwms, small valleys and peat bogs. One of the valleys is Cwm Edno, situated between the ridges of Cerrig Cochion and Yr Arddu. It was above this barren and desolate tract of land that the Dakota, with its captain under the impression that he was flying over the Irish Sea, was caught in a violent downcurrent of air which sent the aircraft into a steep, uncontrollable dive. So sudden was the emergency, the crew did not have time to transmit a Mayday call or provide any details of the situation they faced and the flight ended catastrophically with a high speed vertical dive into a bog in Cwm Edno. There were no survivors of the crash.

And neither were there any witnesses. On that dark, stormy night — a night meant for shelter and the cosy warmth of a fireside — the emptiness of Cwm Edno's bleak, windswept wastes was total, and no human eye observed the grim drama of the Dakota's final, agonised moments. Twenty three people perished inside the metal confines of the aircraft's fuselage as it plunged into that remote mountain bog.

Though the DC-3's demise went unseen, the sound of the stricken airliner's engines was heard in Nant Gwynant and had attracted the attention of the valley's few inhabitants. First to realise that something was wrong was William Williams of Hafod-y-Rhisgl farm, the nearest habitation to the crash site.

That evening, as the wind whistled mournfully around the farmhouse and rain beat against the window panes, he was sitting in his living-room, listening to the radio. Outside, the blackness of the night was absolute, and had imparted a feeling of lonely isolation to the sparsely populated valley, whose small community was made up mostly of farmers such as William Williams. The time was 7.15 p.m. when, suddenly, out of the darkness there came the uneven roar of a low flying aircraft. Thinking that this aerial visitor was in distress, the farmer leapt out of his chair and went to investigate. Almost as soon as he had opened the door, he saw, to his dismay, a vivid flash of light on the hillside south of his farm. He then returned indoors, picked up the telephone and rang the local police to tell them there had been an accident.

Further down Nant Gwynant, a young shepherd, Robert Goronwy Williams of Hafod Lwyfog farm, also heard the Dakota's engines, and he, like his neighbour, was certain something was amiss with the aircraft. The shepherd listened intently for a few seconds as the engine note seemed, to his ears at least, to increase in pitch. There followed the sound of an explosion and as he rushed out into the farmyard he saw flashes of light high on the hillside. Hurriedly putting on his boots and donning warm clothing, he set off through squally rain showers, towards the lights he had just seen. After forty minutes of scrambling over rough ground, with only a small lantern to help him on his way in the inky darkness, he reached the DC-3's wreckage and began to search, without success, for possible survivors. The young man then decided that it was best for him to return to Nant Gwynant as there seemed little point in remaining at the crash site if all the aircraft's occupants were beyond help. Down in the valley he found rescue parties being organised as a result of William Williams' telephone call.

Aware that a very serious accident had taken place and that, in consequence, a large-scale and complicated rescue operation would have to be mounted, numbers of policemen, firemen and RAF Mountain Rescue personnel had gathered, amongst them some high ranking officers including no less a person than the Chief Constable of Gwynedd, who, naturally enough, took control of the operation. The police felt that they were going to be dealing with a major disaster, (though at that stage no-one knew the precise details) and an event of this kind demanded the personal attention of the Force's most senior officer.

Rescue vehicles completely blocked the narrow road that wound its way through the valley, but this did not matter much, as little traffic made use of this particular corridor of communication, especially on a tempestuous night in mid-winter. Amid the vehicles was a fleet of ten ambulances, ready to rush any survivors to hospital.

The first rescue party to set off was guided by Robert Williams, the only person, at that moment, who knew exactly where the Dakota was located. As the men made their way along rough tracks and over boulders, hurricane lamps were left to mark a path for following groups. When Cwm Edno was reached, wreckage could be seen, in the lamplight, scattered over a wide area. The impact had formed a large crater fifteen feet deep, which, because of the boggy ground, was rapidly filling with water. Fire had broken out after the crash but the dampness of the ground, together with the rain that evening, had apparently helped to extinguish the flames quickly. It took only a short time to establish what Robert Williams already knew — there were no survivors. Shortly after midnight, by which hour the cloud and rain had cleared, the Chief Constable decided that nothing more could be done until the morning, when daylight would aid the depressing but necessary job of examining the wreckage and removing the bodies. Everyone returned to Nant Gwynant except a small group of RAF airmen and a few policemen, who stayed behind in order to guard the site. As their colleagues departed, the whole melancholy scene was bathed in the ghostly luminescence of moonlight.

Meanwhile, on the other side of the Irish Sea, staff at Aer Lingus' headquarters were becoming increasingly gloomy as the hours passed and there was no news of the long-overdue DC-3. Some clutched at straws by convincing themselves that Captain Keohane had diverted to another airport, following Captain

Wallace's example, and the aircraft was now safely on the ground, but the total lack of radio contact since the routine call at 7.10 p.m. suggested otherwise. Most of the airline's staff feared the worst, and as the evening wore on, these fears were finally confirmed when news of the tragedy that had befallen the Dakota came through from North Wales.

Immediately, the airline's forceful Assistant General Manager, Captain J.C. Kelly-Rogers began to assemble a team of engineers and accident investigators. Soon, this hastily convened group took off in another of Aer Lingus' Dakotas and flew to RAF Valley, arriving there in the early hours of the 11th. Hustled into waiting transport, they were whisked away to the police station in Bangor, where an Inspector briefed them. Following his advice, the team decided to wait until dawn before going to the crash site.

According to one of the Irish investigators, Richard O'Sullivan, '. . . A grim and desolate sight presented itself', when daylight came to Cwm Edno. He observed that: 'A water filled gash was impressed in the boggy turf.' 'It was the shape of a head-on profile of a DC-3, almost from wingtip to wingtip. In the middle, the telescoped tailplane and fin, all folded into corrugations, protruded slightly, barely evident as parts of an aeroplane.' Inside this crater, the machines' two wings, or rather more accurately, what was left of them had folded back along the fuselage and the lot had concertined and fractured into knife edged fragments. O'Sullivan and his colleagues were not allowed by the police to touch any of the wreckage until the Ministry of Civil Aviation investigators arrived from London. In accordance with international aviation law, theirs was the official responsibility for conducting the crash investigation. This did not, of course, prevent them from co-operating closely with their Irish counterparts.

Soon after examination of the wreckage had begun, a problem arose which seriously hampered the search for vital clues — water was filling the crash crater. Clearly, it would have to be drained, and to this end a pump weighing 1½ cwts was manhandled over rough ground, on 14 January. This pump proved unequal to the task however, and so, on the following day another was taken to the site. With two pumps in operation, the crater was successfully drained.

While British and Irish officials sifted through the wreckage, police and RAF mountain rescue teams removed the bodies of the Dakota's luckless passengers and crew. Of the twenty three bodies, nineteen were recovered, nine of whom could not be identified because they were so badly mutilated, but of the missing four there was not the slightest trace. They had either been hurled so deep into the boggy morass as to be beyond recovery or had suffered complete destruction in the impact.

On Wednesday, 16 January the search for human remains and the smaller pieces of wreckage was ended. Firemen, policemen and RAF personnel had toiled for days in extremely unpleasant conditions, often waist deep in the wet sponginess of the bog. All that was recovered during the day was some luggage and personal belongings which the police hoped would be of assistance to them in the increasingly problematical task of identifying the nine bodies, but unfortunately none of the material proved to be of any use. Indeed, as time passed, and no progress was made in this difficult and harrowing affair, it was becoming apparent that the obstacles to successful identification were insurmountable. The grim puzzle bequeathed by the dead to the living would have to remain forever unsolved.

Eventually, after almost three weeks had elapsed since the disaster, these nine victims were buried at Llanbeblig Cemetery, Caernarfon, on 29 January. In bright sunshine, their plain oak coffins, bearing no inscriptions, were lowered into the ground by police officers. Amongst the mourners was Mr F.H. Boland, the Irish Ambassador, as well as Aer Lingus' most senior executives, and relatives of the dead.

In the case of the four bodies still missing when attempts at locating them were abandoned on the 16th, it was quite obvious that they, or what remained of them, could not be unceremoniously left in a mountain bog. Morality and human decency dictated that appropriate religious rites should be observed, preferably in the form of a Christian burial service. At the very minimum, it would provide some solace for the bereaved families. Accordingly, on 17 January a local Catholic priest, Father James Donnelly of Trefriw, performed what must have been the most unusual interment ceremony of his career. Braving strong winds and a covering of snow on the ground, he, in company with members of the victim's families, climbed up to Cwm Edno, which was as bleak and inhospitable as ever in the cold wind. Standing by the water-filled crater, Father Donnelly delivered a funeral oration for four people of whose identity he could not be sure, and whose final resting place was to be a marsh in a desolate mountain valley, with nothing better than the smashed tail of a DC-3 to serve as their memorial.

Although an inquest was held on 28 January by the Caernarfonshire coroner, it was merely a prelude to the public inquiry, due to be held some months later, in London. No attempt was made at the inquest to answer the all-important question; what had caused the accident? That would have to wait until the public inquiry.

Convened under the authority of the Ministry of Civil Aviation, this inquiry opened on 17 April. It was presided over by J. Roland Adams, QC, sitting with Captain W.B. Caldwell, a BEA pilot, and Mr E. Gold, one of the country's most eminent meteorologists, as assessors. Mr P.S. Bevan acted for the Crown, R. Winn for Aer Lingus and S. Silkin for the passengers' relatives.

It was clear from the start that two factors, icing and turbulence, were to be given a great deal of consideration as possible causes of the crash. After preliminary statements to establish that the Dakota had a valid certificate of airworthiness, was correctly loaded and was flown by a qualified crew, the Inquiry got under way with a formal presentation of the facts, given by Eric Newton, chief aircraft accident investigator at the Ministry. According to him, the DC-3 had gone into a very steep terminal dive, possibly as much as 80°, before the impact. Neither of the engines was found, and only part of the propellers, but from these it was possible to deduce that power was being applied right up to the final moments before hitting the ground. The de-icer control valve had been located and was in the 'on' position. Examination also revealed that part of the starboard wing broke off before impact but no structural defect was evident. Its failure, thought Newton, was probably due to abnormally high stresses imposed by a last minute desperate effort by Captain Keohane and First Officer Newman to pull out of the dive. Newton was certain that wing failure was a consequence of the accident, rather than a cause. Fire was also ruled out as a possible cause.

Turning to the question of the Nefyn beacon, evidence was given by the pilot of another aircraft bound for Dublin on the same night as EI-AFL. He stated that he could identify the beacon but for some reason the needle of his radio compass gave no assistance as regards direction. This, it was thought, might throw some light on Captain Keohane's incorrect report that he was flying over Nefyn.

The Inquiry then moved on to an examination of the cardinal question; was the scale of icing and turbulence experienced on the night of the disaster excessive or not? Evidence was given by a number of pilots that turbulence was severe but not dangerous, and that icing levels varied from soft wet ice to icing so bad that it caused a serious loss of power and airspeed.

Bevan, counsel for the Crown, said the Court would have to decide to what degree the Dakota suffered from the effects of icing and turbulence. If there was icing at 6,500 feet the weather forecast was wrong because it gave the icing level as 8,000 feet and the degree as 'slight rime'. Thus it was vital, Bevan said, to establish how accurate the weather forecast prepared at Northolt had been when it was handed to the Dakota's crew. He was right, of course, and the matter was duly subjected to prolonged and searching analysis, with the help of Joan McKay who, it will be remembered, was the forecaster responsible for providing Captain Keohane with en-route weather information for the flight to Dublin.

On Tuesday 22 April, the spotlight was turned firmly on her, as she spent the day in the witness-box having her professional competence scrutinised in public by lawyers. She was able to deny, with some success, that her forecast was wrong, but at the end of the day's session her interrogators still had not finished with her and on Wednesday she had to resume her seat in the witness-box. When she did so, Counsel for Aer Lingus said, encouragingly: 'The company accepts entirely that you did your job properly and competently and makes no criticism of any kind of your work. On the information you had, we acknowledge that you did your very best.' However, she was then subjected to a further three hours of gruelling cross-examination regarding the quality and accuracy of her work, from which ordeal she emerged with her professional integrity as a weather forecaster unscathed. Indeed, J. Roland Adams said to her: 'Both I and my two assessors (one of whom was a leading expert on meteorology) want to tell you that we have been most impressed with the grasp you have shown of your subject and that you have been a great help to the Court.'

Of significance also was another forecast provided by meteorologist Patrick Canning, on duty at Preston air traffic control centre on the night of the disaster. He told the Inquiry: 'I expected moderate to severe icing over most of the area but I did not foresee severe turbulence *except very locally in the lee of the high peaks of Wales*', (author's italics). Further evidence was given by Eric Newton on the problem of icing. He concluded that from the available evidence it was impossible to determine its effect upon the DC-3's performance. He and his team of investigators could find no direct and conclusive evidence that icing was the cause of the accident.

By mid-May all the witnesses had given their evidence, often facing a barrage of probing questions in the process. The individuals involved ranged from technical experts with sophisticated engineering knowledge, such as Eric Newton, to the shepherd Robert Williams, who had briefly exchanged his bucolic life amidst the tranquil beauty of Nant Gwynant for the noise and bustle of the Metropolis in order to tell the Inquiry, in his strong Welsh tones, of his part in the drama.

Once the formal hearings were over, J. Roland Adams and his two colleagues retired to prepare the report of their findings. By August the eagerly awaited report was ready for publication.

Of the two main causative factors — icing and turbulence — the former was ruled out as the single cause. The Court came to the conclusion that the Dakota crashed because of loss of control brought about when the machine was caught in a powerful downcurrent of air. But although icing had been so firmly rejected, given the strength of evidence presented at the Inquiry surely it could not be completely excluded as a factor in causing control difficulty? Whatever the severity of icing, it was most probably a link in the chain of events that led to disaster. This was the view of some of the accident investigators, both British and Irish, who had participated in the investigation. They felt unable to accept that turbulence alone was responsible for the crash. Convinced that sudden and severe ice accumulation had played a part, they were forced to accept, however, that the villain, as in most cases involving icing, had literally melted from the scene, leaving no evidence whatsoever of its presence.

Three factors were put forward in the report which, either singly or in combination would explain how the accident happened: a) that the pilot, being in error of his true position, began to descend from 6,500 feet to 4,500 feet and ran into an unusually strong downward current of air in the lee of Snowdon, a region of chaotic turbulence from which, in the darkness, it would be extremely difficult to regain control. While he was attempting to do this, the aircraft hit an unusually violent gust which put it completely out of control and broke off the starboard wing, b) that during the turbulence the pilot was dislodged from the controls and could not regain control in time, c) that in the turbulence, movable equipment was dislodged in the cockpit, jamming the controls or injuring the pilot.

But factors b) and c) do not seem very plausible because one would have expected the pilots, as a matter of good airmanship, to have strapped themselves securely in their seats when flying in turbulence. Furthermore, the duplication of controls and the very fact of having two men on the flight deck was expressly designed to prevent the kind of incapacity suggested by factors b) and c).

The report was also critical of Captain Keohane and Flying Officer Newman's navigation in allowing the Dakota to drift twenty miles off track, as this error was a major contributory factor. Although there was no direct evidence as to whether the crew used navigational aids or not, signals from the aircraft suggested no cause for anxiety in the minds of the pilots when they should have been concerned about correcting the excessive drift that was developing.

Some other recommendations made were not unexpected: safety heights for overflying mountains should be related to meteorological data as well as geographical data; that investigations should be made into the nature of air currents in mountain ranges, (see Chapter 16); and that consideration be given to improving channels of communication between airline operators, civil and military aviation authorities to ensure the quickest possible dissemination of weather information to all interested parties. Following the crash of EI-AFL Aer Lingus abandoned the direct route over Snowdon and flights at anything below 6,000 feet when over the Welsh mountains were strongly discouraged thereafter.

During that summer, the crash site in Cwm Edno was fenced off and a few trees planted, to grow as best they could in the harsh mountain climate. Over the years since the accident, remaining wreckage, particularly the tailplane, which was left protruding out of the bog, has attracted many people searching for relics. During the 1980s increasing violation of this site (which, after the service held by Father Donnelly, became consecrated ground) caused some adverse comments to appear in the local press. Disquiet was also expressed by the Catholic community. This led the Snowdonia National Park authorities, in line with their policy of clearing all the aircraft crash sites within the Park's boundaries, to remove every single piece of remaining wreckage from Cwm Edno. Not even the wooden fence was left standing, and all that can be found at the site now is one small, solitary tree, which somehow has managed to survive, against the odds. However, a short distance away, discreetly placed in an inconspicuous position, is a slate memorial plaque which bears the following words:

On The Night Of
10 January 1952
Close To This Vicinity
A C-47 Dakota EI-AFL
The St Kevin Crashed.
All On Board Perished.
R.I.P.

Cwm Edno itself remains unchanged, its remote, bleak landscape as cold and indifferent to the human visitor as ever. The valley, in the aeons of its existence, has seen countless storms of varying degrees of intensity but none have unleashed their fury on this area of barren ground with such tragic consequences as the one which took the lives of twenty three souls on that dark night in January 1952.

Chapter 11

Stranded on Snowdon

Monday, 11 August 1952 was one of the worst summer days experienced in Snowdonia for many years. It began with strong winds, low cloud and heavy rain, which, as the morning hours passed, turned into a severe and unrelenting rainstorm. Most certainly not a day for taking a trip on the Snowdon Mountain Railway — passengers would have tasted nothing of the feast of fine views to be had in good weather — but nevertheless the railway was open for business and had attracted more than 120 people who had decided, despite the inclement conditions, to visit Wales' highest mountain. Two trains, each with over sixty occupants braving wind and rain, had left the railway's Llanberis terminus that morning and embarked upon the toilsome climb to Snowdon's summit, 4½ miles distant and some 3,000 feet higher. Normally, passengers would only have a relatively brief stay at the summit but on this occasion they were destined to spend far longer on the mountain top than anyone had anticipated.

Shortly before 11.30 a.m., with the rainstorm growing steadily worse, the second of the two trains arrived at its destination, thus freeing the single track line for the first train to commence its descent. With driver George Sellars at the locomotive's controls, this train departed from the summit terminus at 11.30 a.m. Blinding rain and thick mist reduced visibility to a few yards, forcing 48 year old Driver Sellars to proceed with the greatest caution. After ten minutes, during which time the train had descended a few hundred feet only, Sellars, while peering through the mist saw, to his amazement, flames on the track some twenty feet ahead. Stopping the train, he and his fireman, Robert Owen, went to investigate.

Blocking the railway line they found the wreckage of an aircraft with its fuselage alight and flames spreading towards the body of a man lying nearby. While the two were in the act of moving the man's body away from the blaze, one of the aircraft's fuel tanks exploded, causing a large burst of flame to erupt from the wreckage. Mindful of the safety of his passengers, Sellars decided to move the train back up the hill, away from the crash, before continuing his search. Soon after, he discovered two more bodies. None of the passengers knew what was happening and were forced to wait anxiously in their locked carriages for some considerable time before being informed of the accident.

Meanwhile, the train's guard, John Roberts, had made his way past the burning debris and walked a quarter of a mile to Clogwyn Halt, from where he was able to telephone Llanberis for help. Luckily, neither the telephone lines or the railway track had been damaged and by midday a trainload of rescuers were on their way: policemen, firemen, the RAF mountain rescue team and two local doctors. There was no life saving to be done however — only the removal of three bodies, brought down the mountain in a railway wagon.

Then there was the problem of the stranded passengers. Obviously, with the line blocked and likely to remain so for many hours, the 11.30 a.m. train could not continue on its downward journey. Driver Sellars had no choice but to reverse his train to the summit, where the sixty passengers rejoined the other group on what would, in all likelihood, be a long wait. At least the summit building, though cheerless, would provide shelter and there was no shortage of food or drink in the cafe.

But exactly what type of aircraft was it which had caused this disruption? Where had the wrecked machine come from and who were the three unfortunate victims of the crash? The answer was to be found at an RAF station on the other side of the Irish Sea, in Northern Ireland. Earlier that morning, 150 miles from rainswept Snowdonia, Avro Anson VM407, laden with stores, had taken off from RAF Aldegrove, near Belfast, on a flight to RAF Llandow in South Wales. Piloting the aircraft was 38 year old Master Pilot J. Malenczuk, a man, as his name suggests, of Polish nationality. He had sixteen years of flying experience to his credit. The comparatively rare rank of 'Master Pilot' held by the Pole was the highest that could be attained by non-commissioned aicrew in the RAF and it indicated tha the holder of this rank was a mature and capable aviator. Malenczuk, who was employed as a pilot with No.23 Maintenance Unit at Aldegrove, had two passengers aboard the Anson: Flight Sergeant J. Tracey and Mr W. Elliott, an Air Ministry civilian employee. The two had no cause to doubt the pilot's abilities — he was known to be held in high regard for his skills by his superiors — but nevertheless, for some unknown reason he submitted an incomplete flight plan that Monday morning for the two hour trip to Llandow.

His intention was to fly under Visual Flight Rules at 2,000 feet — a height to which he could not adhere because of high ground along his route. Furthermore, he had inexplicably failed to obtain weather information for his intended track. At the time of departure — 9.30 a.m. — conditions at Aldegrove were reasonable: visibility at fifteen miles, some scattered cloud at 1,800 feet, more extensive cloud at 8,000 feet, and a light wind. But, as noted, the situation was very different in North Wales, over which the Anson would later be flying.

Within twenty minutes of becoming airborne, Malenczuk ran into cloud thick enough to force him to fly by reference to the aircraft's instruments only. He reported to Aldegrove that he was in IFR (Instrument Flight Rules) conditions at 3,500 feet and then a few minutes later he contacted RAF Valley to request their weather information. Here, conditions were decidedly bad: visibility at one mile, continuous rain, total cloud cover at 3,000 feet with the lowest cloud down to 100 feet, and a 10 knot south westerly wind blowing. In short, a thoroughly unpleasant 'clag' which, as we have already seen, blanketed the whole region.

Then at 10.15 a.m. Malenczuk attempted, unsuccessfully, to contact Llandow. However, his transmissions were overheard at Valley, who, ten minutes later received another request for help from the Anson's pilot. This time he asked if they could ascertain Llandow's weather on his behalf. Valley was able to do so and relayed the information to Malenczuk, who acknowledged this message and also requested the frequency of Llandow Homer (a radio aid to navigation) which Valley, once again, was able to provide. During the next few minutes the pilot was heard calling Llandow but his transmissions were never received there, though why this was the case is something of a mystery. If he was able to communicate with Valley, why not with Llandow? Could the Anson's radio have malfunctioned or perhaps the pilot was mishandling the equipment in some way?

Whatever the reason for these abortive attempts at communication, the Anson continued, throughout, to fly unwaveringly at an altitude of 3,500 feet but the machine had, however, wandered badly off course. It seems that the pilot, distracted by R/T problems, failed to compensate for windspeed and direction. As a result, the aircraft — which was fully serviceable, with its compass swung only three days previously — had been steadily drifting eastwards to such an extent that by the time it was approaching North Wales the deviation from the intended track amounted to twenty five miles, no less. This course, if maintained, would take the Anson straight into the very heart of Snowdonia — the Snowdon massif itself.

But if Malenczuk had flown at the minimum safety height for the area — 5,000 feet — then the fact that he had strayed so far off course would not have become the serious matter that it now was. There would have been time to deal with the communications problem and once radio contact with Llandow had been established then, presumably, the navigational error would, sooner or later, be corrected. By remaining at 3,500 feet the Anson's pilot was putting himself and his two colleagues in mortal danger.

The aircraft was, in fact, heading directly for Snowdon, though the luckless crew had no inkling of this. Thick mist and the rainstorm of that Monday morning ensured they would see nothing beyond the wingtips of their machine. Wrapped in the gloomy greyness of clouds rolling over the unseen hills below, the Anson sped onwards, caught in a situation which had a somewhat paradoxical quality to it. Though the impenetrable vapours cruelly denied even the briefest of life saving glimpses at the rapidly approaching ground, at the same time they served, mercifully, to shield the doomed men from knowing what was about to happen.

Shortly after 10.35 a.m. the Anson flew into the mountain's north west flank, where the ground rises steeply from the dark, brooding cliffs of Clogwyn Du'r Arddu. This is an area of magnificent rock walls and buttresses, renowned among mountaineers for the superb climbing provided but on that rain-soaked day the huge crag was deserted and there were no climbers to witness VM407's crash. The point of impact, five hundred yards from Clogwyn Halt, was slightly below the railway line, on to which the machine then bounced and came to a halt. All three occupants were killed instantly and the aircraft caught fire, the flames of which were later seen by the locomotive driver, George Sellars.

Nobody, it seems, heard or saw the actual collision, though two people did hear the sound of the Anson's engines during its last moments; John Hughes, a railway signalman from Llanberis and Bessie Jones, who worked in the summit cafe. At the subsequent inquest into the accident, she stated that she clearly heard the engines above the roar of the wind, while Hughes said the engine note was uneven, adding that three or four minutes after the aircraft passed, the air was filled with the smell of burning rubber.

On the face of it, this appears to be highly significant evidence suggesting that perhaps some technical failure, or fire even, could account for the crash, but little credence was given to the signalman's statement. As a lay witness, his story could not stand up to the more plausible case put forward by RAF expert witnesses, and his contribution, well meant though it was and no doubt truthfully told, was regarded as something of a red herring.

However, there was supporting evidence though it was not presented at the inquest; a third person also heard the uneven sound of the Anson's engines some minutes before the accident occurred. John Roberts was standing, with his young son William, at a bus-stop outside the village of Bethel, six miles from Llanberis. Father and son were waiting for a bus to take them to Caernarfon when they heard the aircraft overhead. They could see nothing of the machine because of the murk. Roberts turned to his son and remarked: 'There's something wrong with that aircraft — its engines are running rough', a statement which six year old William implicitly took to be true because, after all, his father had been a listening-post operator for anti-aircraft gun batteries during the war and so he should know a great deal about the noise made by aero-engines! Upon reaching Caernarfon, the two were greeted by the wailing of the Fire Service siren (the method then in use to summon auxiliary firemen), a sound which aroused the Roberts' suspicion that the call-out was connected in some way with the aircraft heard earlier by them.

Later, their suspicions were confirmed when they learnt of the Anson's fate. As it so happened, a trip on the Snowdon Railway had already been promised to his son by John Roberts, and so, a week after the crash the two were able to view at close-hand the site of the collision; scorch marks were visible on the rocks and small pieces of wreckage still remained, scattered on the slopes close to the railway track. But would John Roberts' evidence have made any difference to the inquest's outcome if he had testified? It is highly unlikely because the evidence pointing to pilot error was overwhelming: failure to obtain meteorological information prior to the flight, an incomplete flight plan, failure to make full use of R/T facilities available for the purpose of checking his position and lastly, failing to keep to the safety height over the proposed track. Moreover, at no point did the pilot inform Valley — with whom he had no difficulty in communicating — that he was experiencing engine trouble. As we have seen, his sole concern was to establish radio contact with Llandow. Whatever it was that caused signalman John Hughes and ex-soldier John Roberts to think that there was something wrong with VM407's engines, we must assume that both men were mistaken.

As mentioned previously, rescuers were on the scene of the crash by early afternoon. The collision had happened on a part of the track exposed to the full fury of wind and rain, and so bad were conditions the rescue train could go no further than Clogwyn Halt. Had it continued, there was every chance of it being blown over into the precipices of Cwm Glas, which lies immediately to the east of the line at this point. Rescuers were forced to walk the final quarter of a mile, and as one of the group commented: 'We had to fight against rain and a gale when we left the rescue train. We could barely keep our eyes open.' Battered by the unremitting elements, they set about the grim task of removing the bodies, a job made all the worse by the vicious weather. Once the three bodies had been put into a railway wagon, ready for transportation to Llanberis, from where they would be taken to a mortuary in Caernarfon, priority was then given to moving all the wreckage away from the vicinity of the blocked track. This work was completed by 4.30 p.m. and so with the line now clear, it was possible to bring the 120 people stranded on the mountain top back to civilization.

Having spent most of the day cooped up in the dismal summit building, (constructed during World War II as a radar station, though never used as such), the passengers were looking forward to liberation from their unexpected confinement, but it was not to be. Although weather conditions were better than they had been during the morning, the improvement was only slight and in view of this, railway officials decided not to risk bringing the passengers down. They would have to spend the night on the summit, where a howling south westerly gale blew around the small, squat building in which 120 people now resigned themselves to the long evening and night that lay ahead.

While children were kept entertained by comic books and jigsaw puzzles, staff put on an impromptu concert for the adults, including baritone solos by one of the railway guards. There was also dancing to gramophone records by the light of oil lamps. One group of four spent most of the night enthusiastically playing cards but many individuals wanted nothing more than the chance to get some sleep, though for the majority this was difficult, if not impossible. Some managed to doze off on the hard, concrete floor, covering themselves with whatever spare clothing they possessed; others slept fitfully in chairs, while a few had the luxury of mattresses. Youngest of the group was a newly born baby, whose parents came from Essex, and the eldest was a 72 year old Scotsman, Mr James Archibald of Edinburgh, who said of his experience: 'I was quite comfortable in the hotel but the time that we were forced to spend in the train while it was stationary (when the driver first investigated the crash) was an ordeal. We did not know what was happening or what was going to happen.' But neither he or anyone else was any the worse for the trials they endured.

In the summit cafe, manageress Lowri Williams and her assistants kept up a running supply of tea and sandwiches all night for those who wanted them and most people were in good spirits when morning finally came. The sympathetic and kindly railway staff had done an excellent job in maintaining the morale of their customers.

Thankfully, the atrocious weather had abated by dawn and no time was wasted in dispatching two trains to collect the stranded passengers. By 7.30 a.m. they were safely back in Llanberis, where two local hotels, the Royal Victoria and the Padarn Villa, treated them to a free breakfast of bacon and eggs, over which the grateful recipients discussed the accident which had made the last 24 hours a period they would never forget.

During the remainder of the day trains operated normally on the railway, with the two crews from the previous day continuing to work despite their lack of sleep. In fact, business was very brisk with long queues of people forming, most of whom were as eager to view the scene of the Anson's crash as they were to visit Snowdon.

Chapter 12

Bale Out from a V-Bomber

The mighty Vulcan bomber, with its distinctive delta wing was always an impressive sight. On the ground it exuded a sense of menacing potency, a characteristic further revealed when the aircraft flew. Seen in the air, at low level the bomber's massive bulk seemed to overshadow all else, proving even to the most indifferent onlooker that here was a truly awesome war-machine. Becoming airborne was, in itself, a display of sheer, unbridled power. The drama of a Vulcan thundering down the runway on take-off, with its four Olympus jet engines at full throttle was stirring to say the least. A product of the fertile mind of Roy Chadwick (renowned for designing the immortal Avro Lancaster of World War II fame), the Vulcan entered service as a long-range nuclear bomber with the RAF in 1957 though Chadwick himself was not alive to see his innovative design come to fruition. He had been killed in a flying accident in August 1947 at a time when his work on the Vulcan was in the preliminary stages only. The task was completed by fellow designer Stuart Davies.

Undeniably the aircraft was versatile and successful — its longevity is proof enough of that — but it did have one drawback; an inadequate emergency escape system. This system is discussed briefly here as the details are germane to the accident described in the remainder of the chapter. Of the five crew members only the pilot and co-pilot had ejection seats, while their three colleagues, who sat in a windowless compartment behind and below the cockpit, had to make do with conventional parachutes. For these men escape from the aircraft was not easy except in the most favourable circumstances. In fact, this system gave them little chance of survival, particularly at low altitude.

Following a crash in October 1956 at London Airport when the two pilots (one of whom was Air Marshall Sir Harry Broadhurst, Commander in Chief of Bomber Command) ejected to safety, leaving the three others to perish, the Air Ministry was forced to re-consider the question of escape from V-bombers. Technically, it was feasible — but very expensive — to modify the aircraft in order to accommodate extra ejection seats. The Ministry spent twelve months deliberating over the problem before deciding that the Vulcan's escape system would remain unchanged, because, it was said, of the excessive costs involved and the delay in building up the RAF's V-bomber force.

In September 1958 another serious accident took place when Vulcan VX770 crashed during an air display at RAF Syerston, killing seven men — four in the aircraft and three on the ground. Then in August 1959 another V-bomber, a Handley Page Victor, crashed in the sea off the Pembrokeshire coast with the loss of five lives. Many people, including those with much influence in the aviation world were angered by these disasters and voiced their opinions in no uncertain manner. The Air Ministry, accused by its critics of being callous and penny-pinching, was pushed for the second time, and somewhat reluctantly, into continuing the search for an improvement in the Vulcan and Victor emergency escape systems.

By the early 1960s the firm of Handley Page Ltd had devised a system of swivelling seats with inflatable pneumatic cushions which in an emergency would force the seat's occupant to his feet and push him towards the exit. In theory, at least, the time taken to abandon an aircraft would be cut in half. By 1964, while censorious voices were still being heard expressing their dissatisfaction with the new design, a quarter of the bomber force had been modified to take swivel seats, with the remaining 75% due to be modified by the end of 1965.

This was the position, therefore, of V-bomber flight safety when on Thursday 16 July 1964 Vulcan XA909, which had not been modified, took off from its base at RAF Waddington in Lincolnshire. The aircraft belonged to 101 Squadron and was engaged on a navigational training exercise, according to press reports. The flight proceeded normally until XA909 had reached a height of 43,000 feet over Cardigan Bay when an explosion occurred on the aircraft's starboard side. The bomber was some ten miles to the north of Aberystwyth at the time. No fire resulted but cockpit instruments showed that no.3 and no.4 engines had failed and there was also a tendency for the Vulcan to roll to port, which its captain, Flight Lieutenant M.H. Smith corrected by using rudder. It was also discovered that the ailerons were ineffective.

Their control rods had, in fact, been cut by the explosion, though Smith was not aware of this until much later.

There was no doubt about the seriousness of the damage and a Mayday call was transmitted, to which there was an immediate response both from ground stations and aircraft airborne in the area. Co-ordination of efforts to help the Vulcan was carried out by Preston ATC centre, one of the first priorities being to arrange a rendezvous with another aircraft so that an external inspection of the damage could be made. Nearest was one of RAF Valley's Gnats, which was soon on its way. Flight Lieutenant Smith, meanwhile, brought his aircraft down to 10,000 feet, where he levelled out at a speed somewhere between 200 knots and 250 knots. A precise measurement was not possible because the two airspeed indicators were showing different readings.

Although Smith had warned his crew that they might have to bale out, an attempt at a crash landing was the captain's preferred option. His reasoning was simple; if he could get the Vulcan on to the ground with the minimum of further damage then a full technical examination to establish the cause of the explosion would be possible, but if the aircraft was allowed to crash, especially in the sea, the task of accident investigators would be infinitely more difficult.

The nearest airfield was Llanbedr but it was unsuitable for Smith's purpose because the runway was too short and rescue facilities too limited. However, the next airfield — RAF Valley — thirty five miles to the north had runways of sufficient length and a first-rate rescue organisation. It was the obvious choice and so XA909, with its fate hanging in the balance, headed northwards. Much depended on the visual examination of the bomber's external surfaces by the Gnat pilot. One of the crew had already made a limited inspection, using the periscope provided for viewing the aircraft's wings, and discovered damage to the starboard mainplane. This was confirmed by the pilot in the Gnat, who was able to provide further detailed information; there was a large hole, a yard in diameter, underneath the right wing, through which parts of a turbine could be seen, while inspection of the upper wing surface revealed a massive, jagged hole, three feet by ten feet, across the area where the engines were located. Surrounding this hole could be seen several others of varying size, extending on to the spine and port side of the aircraft. It seemed that catastrophic failure of no.3 or no.4 engine had occurred, the explosion from which had also damaged the other engine and the airframe.

But the vital question now was the amount of control of his aircraft available to the captain. Was there enough for him to attempt a landing or not? By using the Gnat, whose airspeed indicator was, of course, functioning correctly, it was possible to establish that the Vulcan would not remain controllable at a speed less than 200 knots. This fact completely dashed Flight Lieutenant Smith's hopes of saving XA909 because landing a weakened machine was far too dangerous at such a high speed. Thus the V-bomber's fate was sealed and Smith had no choice but to inform his crew that the now doomed aircraft would have to be abandoned.

The plan was for the flight to Valley to continue, where the crew would then bale out, leaving the Vulcan to crash. Obviously it would be destroyed in the ensuing impact, following which there would be nothing except bits of twisted metal spread over a large area but there was still a chance that the reason for simultaneous failure of two engines could be ascertained from an examination of the wreckage. Crash investigators were nothing if not extremely thorough and diligent in their work.

Once over Valley, however, Smith had to change his plans yet again when he saw the nature of the airfield's environs. Because the countryside was dotted with so many farms and buildings he realised immediately that his stricken aircraft could not be allowed to crash here. The risk of causing death or injury to civilians was simply too great. If the Vulcan happened to fall on a row of houses, for example, it would wreak havoc and most probably cause large loss of life in addition to extensive destruction of property. To avoid the possibility of such a disaster there was only one course of action left open to Smith and his crew; to bale out over land near the coast and let XA909 head out to sea, and a watery grave.

The V-bomber's captain, in preparation for the coming bale out, set up a practise run at 3,000 feet — judged to be the optimum height for abandoning the machine — over the intended dropping zone, close to Valley. While this rehearsal was taking place, the attendant Gnat, with its ever-watchful pilot, continued to fly in loose formation with the bomber in case some last minute hitch should occur but none did and the dummy run was successfully completed. Then XA909's captain returned to the start of the run and warned the three crewmen sitting behind him that the time for them to jump had finally come.

Inside the confines of their tiny compartment, crammed with electronic equipment, a somewhat anxious trio of aircrew got ready for the moment when they would have to leave their claustrophobic workplace. The three were: Flight Lieutenant A.R. Fraser, navigator (radar), Flight Lieutenant A.W. Houghton, navigator (plotter) and Flying Officer D.M. Evans, air electronics officer.

First, an entry ladder had to be removed from the door in the well of the Vulcan — a job which proved difficult and which took two of the crew to complete. Afterwards, with all three wearing parachutes, helmets and oxygen masks, static lines were connected to the parachutes. When this was done, Flight Lieutenant Fraser reported to the captain that they were now ready to open the door, to which Smith replied by giving the order to do so. Fraser recalled, that: 'On the order to open the door I disconnected my R/T, held the pilot's ladder with my right hand and operated the door with my left. I experienced no difficulty in operating the handle and the door opened immediately. I sat on the door and braced my feet on the jacks. I put my right hand on my manual release and my left hand on my webbing strap. At this time there was very little buffeting, the door providing adequate protection.' So far, so good. Then he had to launch himself into space: 'On bringing my feet together I slid down the door into the slipstream. Here the buffeting was extreme but not unpleasant. I had the impression I was on my back but not tumbling. I made an attempt to pull my manual release but at that moment my parachute deployed.' He landed safely in a meadow near the village of Gwalchmai, some four miles to the east of the airfield, and within minutes he was picked up by one of Valley's rescue helicopters. All his colleagues were also to land on the outskirts of Gwalchmai.

Next to bale out was Flight Lieutenant Houghton, the second navigator. He had watched carefully the progress of his friend and then, he states: 'I followed suit, clamping my oxygen mask on my face and following the exact procedure as carried out by the Navigator Radar.' Houghton left the aircraft cleanly but as soon as he hit the slipstream he began to somersault violently. However, when his parachute deployed, the tumbling stopped and he found himself 'suspended comfortably below the canopy, with no oscillations.' After descending rapidly downwind he landed in the centre of a steeply sloping field. 'I was facing up the hill,' he reported, 'and although I had adopted, as near as possible, the correct landing position, I did not roll over, but collapsed in a heap.' His head struck the ground, breaking the visor on his helmet but otherwise he suffered no physical injury except a few bruises. Shortly afterwards an RAF ambulance arrived and took him to Valley.

Once Houghton had departed from the Vulcan, it was the turn of the Air Electronics Officer, Flying Officer D.M. Evans. He positioned himself at the top of the open door, with his legs braced against the hydraulic jacks. A rubber strip from the door seal was tangled around both jacks and the two navigators' static lines were flapping around on the left of the exit hatch but they did not appear to present any danger. For Evans it was time to go . . . 'I slowly slid down the door,' he said, 'and left the aircraft with my back to the ground.' He maintained this position until his parachute opened. It functioned normally, allowing him an uneventful, swing-free descent. 'There was a great deal of smoke in the sky about a mile on my left,' he observed, 'which, I presumed, came from the crashed aircraft.' Evans' assumption was correct. Immediately below him there was a large hayfield which would be his landing ground. A minute later he hit the earth with more force than anticipated and he found that he had bitten his tongue, which started to bleed slightly. This was his only injury.

With the three rear crewmen having successfully baled out, the co-pilot, Flying Officer G. Woods, was next. He, of course, had the benefit of an ejection seat. After lowering his seat fully, pulling down the visor on his helmet and checking that his harness was as tight as possible, he was ready to go. But first the cockpit canopy, which formed a physical barrier to ejection, had to be removed. The captain gave the order; 'jettison canopy', upon which the two men, acting in unison, grasped the jettison levers and pulled. In a split second the canopy lifted off, producing a marked nose-up change of trim and severe buffeting. 'At this time,' stated Woods, 'we were at 3,200 feet in straight and level flight at about 220 knots indicated — the Gnat pilot was passing us airspeeds throughout the dropping run and in fact told us when each rear crew member's parachute opened.'

Then Flying Officer Woods reached up above his head with both hands for the ejection seat firing handle (which also incorporated a face blind) and yanked it firmly downwards. Instantly he was propelled on a trajectory that took him well above the aircraft. Within a moment or two he heard the bang of the drogue gun which stabilised the seat, his face blind came away and his parachute automatically deployed, leaving the seat to fall to the ground, and destruction. The V-bomber's co-pilot eventually alighted, rather inexpertly, on pasture land. Releasing himself from the parachute harness he looked up and saw a rescue helicopter flying towards him. Luckily, his only injury was a bruised back resulting from the ejection.

Flight Lieutenant Smith was now the sole occupant of the crippled machine. After the canopy had been jettisoned he noticed how intense the sunshine was, even with his visor down; strong light made such a contrast to the dim levels of illumination normally found in a Vulcan cockpit. Immediately Woods had gone, Smith prepared to eject. Sitting up straight, to minimise the risk of spinal damage (the most common form of injury arising from ejection), he pressed his head back hard against the seat and pulled the firing handle but contrary to expectation, nothing happened! There was no explosive upward push, no instant release from the interior of the cockpit, and for one heart-stopping moment Smith thought his seat was not going to fire. He butted his head forward, to no avail, so he pulled his hands further down and butted again. To his immense relief the seat fired and he was shot clear of the bomber.

Shortly afterwards, his parachute opened normally. 'I then looked for the aircraft,' he recollected, 'and saw it about a hundred feet below me, still heading for the sea but with the starboard wing slightly low.' Smith then crossed his arms in front of his face and by pulling on his parachute's lift webs turned round to look for the rest of the crew but he could only see one figure floating down, which he took to be the co-pilot. When the captain turned back, XA909 had started a shallow dive and was flying towards the airfield at Valley. 'For a few moments,' the pilot said, 'I was afraid it might hit the airfield but I soon realised that its dive was becoming steeper and that it would crash before it got there.' Hanging from the straps of his parachute, Flight Lieutenant Smith watched the final moments of his aircraft, as its dive became ever steeper until it crashed near Gwalchmai.

Having seen the Vulcan disintegrate, Smith then turned his attention to the immediate problem of making a good landing. He was six hundred feet above the ground and heading for a large field but being rather inexperienced in making parachute landings he misjudged his height and instead of staying relaxed, he braced himself. Consequently, when he hit the ground, the impact was so hard that he was dazed though he quickly regained his senses when he found that he was being dragged along the field by his still open parachute. To prevent this he banged the quick release box on his harness but was only partly freed from the straps as his left leg remained entangled. Still being hauled along the ground, he attempted to collapse the parachute canopy by rolling on his stomach and pulling in the rigging lines. This had the desired effect and the canopy collapsed almost at once. Ten yards away a rescue helicopter landed and picked up Smith. His injuries were found to be minor: a slight nose bleed, a cut near his right eye and bruising. Soon he was able to rejoin his crew at RAF Valley, where they were being taken care of in the station's sick quarters.

Without doubt the five men had been extremely lucky to have escaped, more or less uninjured, from their damaged machine — the first crew to do so from a Vulcan, apparently. In their favour they had the enormous advantage of time. If any one factor had ensured their survival, this was surely it. After the explosion in its engines, the V-bomber had remained firmly airborne and though control was impaired, most fortunately, the impairment was only partial, which meant that straight and level flight — a very important ability — was still possible. This had given the crew vital time to prepare for a bale out, which was then executed in ideal conditions and with the added luxury of another aircraft flying alongside to provide guidance.

But if control loss had been total or become progressively worse then XA909 would have probably spiralled down to the ground, with G-forces building up and creating virtually insuperable difficulties for the crew members without ejection seats, thereby eliminating any hope of escape for them. The Fates had been more than kind to three RAF officers that day.

So much for the drama in the air. What had been happening on the ground meanwhile? Very little, at least up to that point, except at Valley, where there was much activity as the station's Search and Rescue unit — 'C' Flight of 22 Squadron — with its yellow painted Whirlwind helicopters, sprang into action in company with the emergency and medical services. A few miles away, the inhabitants of Gwalchmai had no inkling of what was taking place in the sky above their homes or what was about to happen. However, the situation soon changed when the V-bomber took its final earthward plunge a mile to the west of the village. First to notice that something was amiss were startled motorists on the nearby A5 road, who saw parachutes floating down in the afternoon sunshine, quickly followed, to the onlookers' amazement, by a Vulcan — its huge delta winged form quite unmistakable — heading directly towards the ground.

The aircraft, with its starboard wing well down, flew over the A5 and across an adjoining field, narrowly missing power lines in the process. In this field a number of small, rocky outcrops were to be found, one of which was responsible for bringing about the demise of XA909. The machine's starboard wing caught this particular outcrop and as a result the Vulcan was sent cartwheeling into the next field, where it exploded in a ball of fire. Had the rocky hump not been there, then the V-bomber, to judge from its flight path, would have continued unhindered until it met the next obstruction, a few hundred yards ahead; a large house belonging to the farm of Treddolphin. On the eastern side of the farmhouse, placed immediately between it and the approaching aircraft, there grew a band of stout, mature trees which would have taken the brunt of an impact, had it occurred. But even so, with an aircraft the size of the Vulcan the forces involved were tremendous and in all probability the house would have suffered some degree of damage. It had one occupant — an elderly woman — at the time of the crash.

She was the mother-in-law of farmer Hugh Williams, owner of Treddolphin and upon whose land XA909 now lay in countless fragments. That Thursday had been just another normal, working day for Hugh Williams, but the afternoon's events would make it into a day he would never forget. After lunch he had gone to one of the farm's outbuildings to dose some ewes with medicine. Sheep can be tiresomely un-cooperative creatures at the best of times but nevertheless the farmer, with help from his wife, was making good progress when their work was suddenly interrupted by the frightening sound of a huge, earth-shaking explosion close by. Thoroughly alarmed, the pair rushed out into the open, to be greeted by an astounding sight; one of their fields was almost completely covered by a mass of burning, smoking wreckage.

Hugh Williams took only a few moments to recover from his initial surprise. Realising that an aircraft had crashed on his land he instinctively ran to the burning debris and started to look for survivors. His search was totally unnecessary, though he was not to know. Later the farmer, somewhat to his bewilderment (and annoyance) was admonished by the RAF for taking this action. What to him had been a simple desire to help any injured victims of the crash was regarded by the military authorities as a pointless act which was also full of risk. According to them, explosions could have occurred in the wreckage at any time and Williams was in grave danger of becoming a casualty or even losing his life.

Be that as it may, in the immediate aftermath of the Vulcan's destruction another problem arose for the unfortunate man; his field soon became the focus of attention for a great number of people. Drawn as if by some irresistibly powerful force, they came hurrying from every direction: across meadows, along lanes, over walls and hedges, each person with but one aim — to reach the scene of the crash as quickly as possible. Gates were left open, livestock was stampeded and cars abandoned on the A5 road as their drivers joined the crowd of villagers and others, all converging on Treddolphin, where Hugh Williams watched, with mounting anxiety, the mass invasion of his farm. Scarcely able to believe that, in his own words: 'So many people could appear, apparently from nowhere, in such a short space of time,' he had no means of restraining the throng as they swarmed over his land. He decided, very sensibly, to telephone the police, who arrived with commendable speed probably because they had already been informed of the crash and its location by the RAF. To Hugh Williams' relief, the police were most efficient in setting up a cordon around the site. Additionally, all the roads were closed.

This prompt action ensured the minimum of disruption to the wreckage by souvenir hunters and also prevented any further damage to Treddolphin.

As noted already, XA909's violent end brought very little injury to humans, a happy situation which applied equally to livestock in the immediate area of the crash. Only two animals were affected: a solitary sheep and a bull. Pieces of metal from the explosion had hit the sheep but the resultant wounds were superficial and not serious in any way — a fact which pleased the Williams' greatly because the ewe in question was more of a pet to them than anything else, and upon whom they had bestowed the name of 'Glenys'. In the case of the second victim, a Hereford bull, a different kind of suffering was inflicted upon the animal. Massive strength, virility and aggressiveness are the qualities normally associated with bulls, but such was the terrifying spectacle of the Vulcan's explosive disentegration that this particular one, though not physically harmed in the least, was reduced to a state of continuous, uncontrollable trembling. According to veterinary opinion the afflicted bull was so badly shocked that it had experienced the bovine equivalent of a nervous collapse!

Much later that day, when the hubbub had died down, a theft of livestock was discovered when Hugh Williams found that some of his lambs were missing from a pen — stolen by an opportunist thief, presumably a farmer, during the confusion caused by the afternoon's events. The robber was never caught.

Initially, the civilian police exercised control at the crash site but soon they were able to hand over to the RAF. A guard was mounted over the wreckage by airmen, with welcome refreshments kindly provided for them by Mrs Williams, the farmer's wife, who took pity on the men when she learnt that they had not been issued with rations. Over the next few days debris in abundance was gathered and heaped in large piles, ready for loading on to lorries, for which task a crane was necessary. Hugh Williams noticed that these piles were located close to the power lines which XA909 had so narrowly missed. The choice of this location was evidence of thoughtlessness on someone's part, reflected the farmer, considering that the material was to be handled by a crane; accidental contact with the overhead cables was so obvious a danger. Expecting sparks to fly, literally, he watched the proceedings with interest; sure enough, no sooner had the crane arrived than its jib touched the power lines, causing loss of the electricity supply to Treddolphin, all the surrounding farms and part of Gwalchmai. Three weeks were to pass before the RAF finally departed.

The tons of wreckage removed from the farmer's field was now nothing more than scrap and of no interest to those whose job it was to investigate the crash. They concentrated on the aircraft's two starboard engines, whose failure had so clearly precipitated the drama that followed. But the question — and it was a vitally important one — was why the two Olympus engines, normally so reliable, had failed *simultaneously*? Technical experts examined what remained of the pair and were able to provide an answer; a bearing failure in no.4 engine was the root cause of trouble. After this bearing had fractured, an explosive disintegration of the low-pressure turbine disc took place. Fragments of this disc and its casing were then blasted with great force, like pieces of shrapnel from a shell, into the neighbouring no.3 engine causing its immediate failure, with the consequences that have been described.

The outcome of the Vulcan's unexpected end on that Thursday afternoon, given that a destructive and fiery collision with the ground was inevitable and that its precise location had to be left to chance, was as satisfactory as it could possibly have been; no loss of life and minimal damage to property. Even the pain endured by Hugh Williams' animals — the Hereford bull and Glenys the pet sheep — was only temporary, and it is pleasing to record that both made a full recovery. Indeed, Glenys, after giving birth to fine lambs year after year, lived to a ripe old age!

Chapter 13

Helicopter Fatality

For eleven years, from 1968 until 1979, there were no helicopter accidents in Gwynedd and it seemed, as the 1970s drew to a close, the decade would pass without any such incident, but it was not to be. In the autumn of 1979 the possibility of an accident-free decade was destroyed by two fatal crashes which occurred within a few weeks of each other.

The first took place at Rhos-goch, near the small port of Amlwch on Anglesey's northern coast. Here the giant multinational oil company, Shell, had built a marine terminal in the 1960s to offload crude oil from supertankers into storage tanks at Rhos-goch, three miles away. The oil was then pumped through an underground pipeline which ran across Anglesey to the mainland and along the North Wales coast to the company's refinery at Stanlow, in Cheshire.

This pipeline, in common with all such installations, needed periodic inspection, for which purpose helicopters had been used because of the speed and ease with which they could carry out the work. If the reader is a little puzzled as to why and how an underground pipeline could be inspected, there were two main checks to be carried out. First, to ensure that no violation by landowners of the pipeline easements had taken place. These easements were agreed at the time of construction and they restricted access to, and work, in the immediate area of the pipeline. It was important for Shell that the agreements be strictly adhered to. The second function of the airborne inspection was to look for any changes in the vegetation along the route as this would indicate the early stages of a leak.

On Thursday, 25 October 1979, shortly after 9.30 a.m. a Hughes 269C helicopter landed on the helipad at Shell's Rhos-goch site in order to pick up a company employee, whose duties that day included the pipeline's regular fortnightly inspection. The two seater helicopter, registered G-BBIU, and owned by a firm in Leeds was flown by a 22 year old pilot with 500 hours of flying experience, 250 of which were on helicopters. His passenger was a local man from the nearby village of Pen-y-sarn who, besides his work for Shell, was also making a name for himself as a singer and entertainer, having appeared a number of times on Welsh television. However, as he settled into his seat and tightened the harness straps (whose deficiencies would soon be revealed) he did not know that he had only a few seconds left to live.

The start of the pipeline, where the inspection would also begin, was at a point 400 metres from where the helicopter stood. Its pilot, who had been to Rhos-goch three times previously, could choose to reach the starting point by either a direct or indirect take-off path and seems, logically enough, to have selected a direct route to the pipeline, but across the chosen path there ran a line of high-voltage power cables, 180 metres distant and a few metres higher than the take-off point.

These cables, to quote the Department of Trade's Accident Investigation Branch bulletin (no. 3/80) '. . . were not easy to see against the background of a small ridge.' This is something of an understatement because the power lines are well nigh impossible to see. Viewed from the helipad they are below the skyline and are hidden so effectively by fields and the green foliage of hedges as to become practically invisible. Furthermore, because of local topography — the ground slopes downwards from the oil tank site entrance to the pylons — there was very little height difference between the helipad and the cables at their lowest point. They were, in fact, almost level with the helipad and in a position a pilot would not have expected power lines to be. The supporting pylons, on the other hand, were easily discernible.

After the Shell employee had boarded the helicopter it lifted off normally and hover-taxied slowly for 50 metres before accelerating away but its flight came to an abrupt and catastrophic end when the machine flew directly into the power lines. No attempt was made to climb over them and there is no doubt the pilot had not seen the danger which lay ahead. After the collision G-BBIU broke up and fell to the ground, throwing both men clear of the wreckage. The passenger was already dead — he had been killed instantly — while his colleague was very badly injured.

First on the scene were firefighters from the Shell site followed soon after by members of the Gwynedd Fire Service. Although fuel had leaked from the wrecked helicopter there was no fire, much to the relief of the site's manager. The last thing he would have wanted was a fire anywhere in the vicinity of tanks where 700,000 cubic metres of crude oil was stored. Two Wessex helicopters from RAF Valley also arrived at Rhos-goch. On board one was the station's medical officer, who spent fifteen minutes trying to resuscitate the injured pilot with little success. The pilot was then airlifted to hospital in Bangor, where he later died.

Accident investigators who examined the wreckage discovered that the victims were thrown from their seats because the quick-release fastenings of their harnesses became undone during the impact, but even if the fastenings had held, it would not have made any difference to the outcome. Pathological evidence indicated that the accident was not survivable. The harnesses were fitted to the helicopter in 1978 in accordance with a Civil Aviation Authority requirement for upper torso restraint but the crash had, rightly so, led to close scrutiny of the design and the subsequent discovery of its shortcomings. As a result, the CAA issued what is known as an EAAD (Emergency Additional Airworthiness Directive) which required all operators of similar helicopters (the Hughes 269 and 369 series) to replace the faulty buckles or complete harness with those of a different design.

In modern times the increasing profusion of power lines has become a great hazard for aviators, particularly those who fly regularly at low level. Electricity cables and pylons can be very difficult to see, especially if the light is poor or there is haze. In these conditions, power lines can merge into the background completely — an invisible but deadly trap for the unwary. Undoubtedly, speed is often a contributory factor where the pilot has little or no opportunity to see the approaching danger, but in this particular accident it did not apply. The helicopter's pilot had landed at the oil storage site, with which he was familiar from previous visits, had then taken off and moved slowly towards the cables, only a short distance ahead, yet neither he or his passenger, apparently, saw anything of the power lines and neither did they spot the visual clue provided by the pylons — a clue which might well have saved them from the disaster they had swept headlong into.

Then, only three weeks after this tragedy another took place, again involving a Hughes 269C helicopter and electricity cables, though on this occasion the cables were not the direct cause of the accident.

On Monday, 12 November helicopter G-CHIC was on hire to the Merseyside and North Wales Electricity Board, (MANWEB), for the purpose of checking the condition of power lines in North Wales. The inspection was being carried out, over a two day period, by a MANWEB engineer while the helicopter was flown by an experienced pilot, 44 years old and with nearly 1,200 flying hours entered in his logbook. The day passed without incident and in the evening the two men, between whom a friendship had developed as a result of a number of previous flights of this nature, returned to their starting point at Chester, where the Electricity Board's head office was located and where the helicopter was parked overnight, in the open. On the following day, at 9.25 a.m., after experiencing some difficulty in starting the helicopter's engine, which the pilot attributed to the battery state, the pair were once again airborne in G-CHIC and heading for North Wales to continue their task.

At 11.00 a.m., following an uneventful and trouble-free period of inspection work, they arrived at the attractive little town of Betws-y-coed, one of Snowdonia's most popular tourist spots. During the summer months holidaymakers had thronged the streets in their thousands but now, in mid-November, with the tourist season well and truly over, the mountain resort was empty and cold. Despite sunshine, the air temperature that morning was little more than a chilly 3°C.

Shortly after 11.00 a.m. the helicopter's pilot flew towards a small flat-topped rock outcrop known as Clogwyn-y-Cyrau, immediately to the north of the town. This plateau-like outcrop formed a convenient landing pad and when G-CHIC's engine was switched off, bringing the rotor blades slowly to a halt, the two men relaxed as they took their mid-morning break. During the break they watched, with interest, a group of climbers on a cliff nearby.

After twenty minutes it was time to return to work but then the helicopter's engine refused to start and failed to fire on the second and third attempts, a fact which the pilot (mistakenly) assumed to be the fault, once again, of the aircraft's battery. However, on the fourth try the engine burst into life and appeared to run normally. Rotor engagement, run-up and take-off to a low hover of two feet above the rock plateau was also satisfactory. Fifteen seconds later, as the helicopter began to move off, the transition from hover to forward flight unexpectedly faltered. The machine did not gain height and speed as it should have, remaining unresponsive to increasingly large control inputs made by the pilot. 'There's something wrong with the controls,' he shouted to his colleague as he struggled with the cyclic stick and yaw pedals, but to no effect. The MANWEB engineer, who could not hear anything unusual in the engine note or detect an excessive vibration level, watched with extreme apprehension as the pilot fought a losing battle to gain control of his machine.

By now the helicopter's skids were clear of the rock plateau, which fell away on all sides. To the north was the edge of a pine forest, while a short distance from the western side of the outcrop — in which direction the attempted take-off was taking place — there was an obstruction in the form of a birch tree. The top of this tree protruded a few feet above the level of the landing site. Following loss of control the machine's nose dropped as it lost height and drifted in a yawing manner to starboard before striking some pine trees and crashing to the ground, twenty feet below. When the helicopter finally came to rest, with its engine still running, it was in a 90° nose down attitude.

Inside the machine, its pilot lay injured and unconscious while the engineer had escaped with nothing worse than a cut on his hand, though he was badly shocked. Nevertheless, seeing that his friend was hurt he tried to help but failed to free him from his seat. He then attempted, successfully, to switch off the engine although he was aware that something continued to make a noise and he noticed an illuminated switch marked 'gearbox' flashing on the instrument panel.

Meanwhile, the group of climbers — soldiers, in fact, engaged on a mountain training exercise — having witnessed G-CHIC's disastrous plunge to the ground, abandoned their rock-climbing and dashed across to render assistance. They removed the still unconscious pilot from the wreckage and, displaying good soldierly initiative, the men improvised a stretcher from available materials to carry the pilot down to lower ground. Soon the crash victims were being whisked away in an ambulance to hospital in Llandudno. Sadly however, the pilot was dead on arrival; his skull was fractured and the resultant haemorrhage proved fatal. He was not wearing a protective helmet but if he had done so, he would probably have survived. His colleague was much luckier; after being treated for shock he was released from hospital a few hours later.

When investigators from the Department of Trade arrived at Betws-y-coed and conducted an on-site examination of the wreckage they were able to construct a sequence of events which showed that the helicopter's main rotor had struck the pine trees and the tail rotor, at some stage during the accident, had collided with the birch tree. Impact marks indicated the machine had a low forward speed and was turning to the right when it crashed. The tail rotor had separated from its drive shaft but the attachment bolt could not be found, thereby making it impossible for the investigators to be certain whether the bolt had come out because of the impact or by virtue of some other cause. Clearly, this was an important point as the loss of this small but vital piece of steel could be the primary reason for the crash. The investigating team succeeded, however, in establishing to their satisfaction that the bolt had remained intact until the moment of impact. The team's enquiries, which embraced all the paperwork relating to G-CHIC, revealed that four weeks before the accident the pilot had attempted to remove the tail rotor assembly so that it could be repainted. He failed in this attempt and later flew the helicopter to an aircraft engineering company, where the repainting work was done. This included removing the blades and respraying, refitting and balancing them. The tail rotor hub attachment bolt was not disturbed, and furthermore, it was noticed that it had been split-pinned. It was almost certain, therefore, that tail rotor damage was a result and not a cause of the accident.

So what other factor or set of factors could have been responsible for the crash? After examination of the rest of the wreckage had failed to disclose any evidence of pre-crash malfunction or jamming of the flying controls, the finger of suspicion pointed at the helicopter's 190 h.p. Lycoming engine. It was removed from the site and taken to the Royal Aerospace Establishment at Farnborough, where it was subjected to rigorous testing which showed an approximate power loss of 26% in the unit. Further investigation revealed that over half of this loss was caused by dirty spark plugs. The maintenance schedule stated that these items were to be cleaned or replaced after every 100 hours of operation but G-CHIC had completed 120 hours since the last recorded servicing of its spark plugs.

This was the root cause of the accident. The pilot had only three quarters of the engine power normally available to him, and this limited amount of power was not sufficient to prevent the helicopter from drifting helplessly into trees near the rock plateau. But given the circumstances in which the emergency arose, it is fair to ask the question; could more have been done to prevent the flight from ending in the grievous way that it did? The answer, probably, is no. Perhaps if the pilot had had a little more time to assess the position he found himself in, or if the area surrounding the plateau was more level and with fewer obstructions, then it might have been possible to get the rapidly failing machine back on the ground safely, thus averting a crash, but this is conjecture only. One point is clear, however; Clogwyn-y-Cyrau, though convenient for temporary use on that morning, proved to have fatal shortcomings as a helicopter landing pad.

Chapter 14

Mid-air Collision over Carmel

In November 1962 a new type of aircraft arrived at RAF Valley to replace the Vampires which had served so well for ten years and more. The replacement was the Hawker Siddeley Gnat, a diminutive swept-wing aircraft developed originally as a fighter and subsequently adapted for flying training purposes. Of the 105 Gnats delivered to the RAF, most went to Valley, which by the time deliveries were completed in August 1963, possessed a fleet of 89 aircraft. Once in service, the Gnat turned out to be rather disappointing, however. While its light responsive controls made it exhilarating to fly, it lacked stability and could be something of a handful, not only for the less adept student pilots but also for experienced instructors. The hydraulically operated control system was complex and not always reliable, with the tailplane proving to be especially troublesome. It was prone to sudden failure and became something of an Achilles' heel for the Gnat. The engineering problems involved were difficult to overcome and in fact were never properly solved.

Another disappointment was the accident rate. From July 1964 onwards a number of aircraft were lost, mainly due to failure of the intricate hydraulic system, though technical malfunction was not the sole reason for every loss suffered. As one would expect at a flying training school, human error on the part of those who flew the aircraft accounted for some accidents, and it is one such example whose details are described here.

This particular accident happened in 1965, a year which saw RAF Valley's safety record take a battering, with no less than six crashes — an average of one every two months — casting a shadow over the year's achievements. Of the six accidents, the fourth was the most serious, resulting in the deaths of two pilots, injury to a third, and the destruction of two aircraft.

The events in question occurred on the morning of Thursday, 22 April when a trio of Gnats took off from the airfield on a formation flying exercise. Leading the formation, in Gnat XR950, was one of Valley's flying instructors, accompanied by a colleague in the rear cockpit. This second man had no official part in the flight, having gone along merely in order to maximise his flying experience. As their wingmen they had two student pilots, one of whom was in Gnat XS108, an aircraft which had been at Valley for two months only. It was destined to have a brief career.

Shortly before 11.00 a.m. the three aircraft were flying in formation a few miles south of Caernarfon when a collision took place between the leading Gnat and XS108. Its pilot had been ordered to close in on the leader, but unfortunately he did so with slightly too much speed, and as a result his machine touched the other. Both were damaged by the encounter, with the lead aircraft coming off worst. To judge by subsequent events it quickly became uncontrollable while the second Gnat, on the other hand, remained sufficiently intact for its student pilot to nurse it back to Valley.

He managed to reach the runway threshold only to find that his aircraft was threatening to stall at its normal landing speed, no doubt because of the damage it had sustained, and so touch-down was at a much faster pace than usual, a pace so rapid that the pilot lost control and crashed. Sadly, he received fatal injuries and died while being taken to hospital.

His fellow student in the undamaged Gnat had, meanwhile, flown to the RAF's second airfield on Anglesey — RAF Mona — where he landed safely. As the aircraft's wheels rolled along Mona's single runway the pilot must have wondered what had become of the others in the flight. While he knew XS108 had attempted a landing at Valley (but did not know the tragic outcome) he had no idea what was the fate of the third machine, XR950. It was, in fact, nothing more than a heap of pulverised, shattered material, completely unrecognizable as an aircraft. With serious harm inflicted upon it by the collision, XR950 had gone into a dive from which it did not recover before hitting the ground. As for the two men on board, one — the occupant of the rear cockpit — had ejected successfully, though breaking his leg in doing so. He landed on farmland near the village of Carmel, five miles south of Caernarfon, and while he was now out of danger, his friend was not. For some reason he failed to eject and remained in the doomed Gnat as it entered its terminal dive.

Beneath the aircraft, as it swiftly lost height, lay Carmel, quiet and peaceful in the morning sunshine. It is a typical upland village of the region, with a close-knit Welsh community whose livelihood, in the past, depended almost entirely upon the nearby slate quarries of Nantlle. Poverty and deprivation was the lot of many families but this bred strong ties between those who alleviated their hardship by means of mutual sharing and support. While slate quarrying and the grinding poverty of the past has long since disappeared, a strong sense of community remains among Welsh people living in this area.

The sound of jet engines was heard frequently here, as military aircraft were to be seen regularly flying to and from the mountains close by, but the jet noise heard by Carmel's inhabitants on that Thursday was very unusual because it was suddenly interrupted by a bang and then followed by a whine which grew increasingly louder. Some people were outdoors when they heard the sound, among them Mona Jones, secretary of the local Women's Institute branch. Mrs Jones was walking at that moment, in company with her young daughter, the quarter mile from the village to their cottage. On hearing the strange noise above them, they looked upwards and saw, to their surprise, an aircraft diving steeply towards the ground. Mother and daughter watched in horror as the machine hurtled downwards, until it crashed into a small field at a place known as Bwlch-y-llyn, one mile from Carmel. As can be imagined, the impact generated extremely destructive forces which killed the pilot instantly and totally destroyed his aircraft in an explosion that sent earth and stones showering over the surrounding land.

Some fifty yards from the point of impact stood two houses which were shaken by the blast, resulting in some broken windows, though luckily no serious damage was done. Inside the houses, however, their occupants were almost reduced to a state of terror; one woman was in her kitchen when the Gnat passed overhead so closely that she thought the roof was collapsing, while her thirteen year old daughter screamed with fright at the deafening noise. They ran from the kitchen and saw that a covering of soil and stones lay on the hallway floor, (the front door was open at the time of the explosion). Their neighbour was a frail and elderly man not in the best of health and on that day was confined to bed because of illness. Already in a weakened condition, the unfortunate man was greatly distressed and shocked by what had happened. It is said that he never fully recovered from the shock. Others who came rushing to the scene, hoping to assist any survivors, could not see anything except a large, deep crater in the ground surrounded by pieces of wreckage, some of which were burning.

Meanwhile, at Valley the emergency services found themselves in something of a rescuer's nightmare, with two accidents to deal with simultaneously and a number of casualties/survivors to pick up, all in different geographical locations. While the crash of Gnat XS108 on the airfield meant that medical staff were on the scene immediately, this was not so in the case of the other aircraft. Some confusion arose over the precise location of the accident and as it took time for all the details to be pieced together the effect was to hamper efficient action. For instance, it was mistakenly thought at the start of the rescue operation that the pilots had baled out over the sea, causing a large sea-search to be mounted, with local lifeboats launched and Shackleton aircraft from Ballykelly in Northern Ireland sent to assist. In fact, coping with this double emergency extended Valley's rescue and medical facilities to their limits, but once the picture became clear, the familiar yellow helicopters of 'C' Flight, 22 Squadron, were quickly on their way to Carmel.

Those in charge of the operation assumed that both of the Gnat's occupants had ejected and while the second pilot was found without too much difficulty, by means of the radio homing beacon which formed part of his survival kit, searchers were somewhat nonplussed by their inability to discover the whereabouts of his colleague until they realised that he was still inside the aircraft when it crashed. But why did he, and indeed the student pilot involved in this tragic accident, fail to eject when they had the opportunity to do so? Their chances of survival would have been vastly increased, if not positively guaranteed, yet both chose to remain with their aircraft until the end.

In the case of the student, he clearly retained sufficient control over his machine to reach Valley, where the problem of landing the damaged Gnat proved too much, with disastrous results, as we have seen. This prompts the question; was there anything at all to be gained from attempting a landing in these critical

148

circumstances? The obvious answer was the saving of one rather expensive aircraft for the RAF, though at the risk of losing both pilot and aircraft if the gamble did not come off.

It can be safely assumed that the young pilot had not been acting entirely on his own initiative, because he would almost certainly have received a great deal of advice from his superior officers, who, once they were informed of the mid-air collision, would have gathered without a moment's delay in Valley's control tower to supervise and co-ordinate the handling of the resultant emergency. How the decision to try for a landing was reached or who took it is not known, but in the event it proved to be an erroneous action, though it is easy to say this with the benefit of hindsight. If the pilot had ejected, then the only loss would have been that of the aircraft.

The case of the luckless flight leader is not quite so clear-cut, however. His failure to eject cannot be explained with complete certainty because any evidence which might have thrown light on the matter was destroyed in the crash. But it is possible to deduce from the known facts — though admittedly an element of conjecture is involved — that collision damage may have prevented the pilot from firing his seat, thus imprisoning him in the cockpit. It is also possible that he could have been incapacitated by injury or loss of consciousness.

The residents of Carmel were convinced that he had deliberately sacrificed his life to prevent his aircraft from falling on their village, but this claim cannot, in all honesty, be substantiated. With the strictly limited amount of information available, it is simply not possible to ascertain how controllable the Gnat was during those last moments. The fact that the crash site was located outside the village does not, of itself, necessarily mean that the aircraft was steered to that particular spot in order to avoid hitting buildings — chance is as equally valid an explanation as human choice for the impact to have occurred in that small field. The full facts could not be established then, nor can they now or indeed in the future. Given the paucity of evidence, the villager's claims cannot be proved or disproved. The matter is beyond enquiry and will forever remain so.

But one aspect of the tragedy never in any doubt was the extent of Carmel's sympathy with the pilot's wife and two young sons. As a token of this sympathy and in accordance with the tradition of the slate quarrying communities, a sum of money was collected and sent to the bereaved family. The task of forwarding this money was entrusted to Mona Jones, who, as noted previously, had been one of the witnesses to the crash. Somewhat unexpectedly, the money was returned by the pilot's widow with a request that it be used to plant willow trees at the place where her husband died, but her wishes could not be complied with because, as experts pointed out, trees of this variety would not grow in the poor soil and harsh climate of this upland area. Indeed, it is not a good place to plant trees of any kind, as their absence from the landscape testifies.

With the question of what to do with the money unresolved, in time-honoured fashion a committee was set up to deal with the matter. After some discussion, the committee proposed that the money be used to erect two public seats in the village, and as this suggestion was acceptable to all interested parties, the seats, made of concrete and wood, were duly built on a piece of land in front of the local chapel. The site commands an excellent view of the surrounding scenery; mountains to the south west, then the wide sweep of Caernarfon Bay with the flatter prospect of Anglesey beyond, and as such, the location cannot be bettered.

On a bitterly cold Sunday in March 1967 a special bi-lingual service in memory of the dead pilot was held in Carmel's chapel, after which the congregation of 150 people filed out of the building and gathered around the two seats just a few yards away while a brief ceremony of dedication took place. The service ended with this staunchly Welsh congregation singing a hymn in English, something not normally done but they did so on this occasion as a mark of respect for the man who had lost his life so tragically in this small and peaceful village. By their actions, the residents of Carmel had demonstrated a deep vein of compassion and humanity. This compassion, rooted in the adversities and dangers of the slate quarrying past, remains to this day as an admirable feature of life in this upland community.

Chapter 15

Incident in Cwm Penmachno

In the previous chapter, reference has been made to the difficulties which arose after the Gnat advanced jet trainer entered into service with No. 4 FTS at RAF Valley in the early 1960s. A high accident rate, on the one hand, and a low serviceability rate on the other, coupled with technical problems conspired to disrupt the all-important flying training schedules. Although 4 FTS' instructors and engineers tried to overcome the difficulties and disappointments as best they could, inevitably there was some lowering of efficiency. The situation was so unsatisfactory by the mid-1960s that a determined effort to improve matters was embarked upon, and as a result extra resources were allocated to Valley. Another training squadron was to be formed, bringing the total to three, and the Gnat fleet was to be augmented by Hawker Hunter aircraft, which the new squadron would operate.

By early 1967 the Hunters were in residence. Two variants were flown; the single seat F.6 with its strikingly clean lines, and the T.7, a two-seat dual control trainer. While the T.7 was a fine, attractive looking aircraft, it did not match the near-perfect symmetry of the sleek single seater — one of the most beautiful jet fighters ever built, some would argue — but nevertheless the T.7 successfully did the job it had been designed to do.

Besides relieving the pressure caused by Gnat unserviceability, the Hunters were additionally utilised to train the many student pilots who came to Valley from Commonwealth and foreign air forces — Australia, Singapore, Jordan and Lebanon, for example. Unhappily, it was a young Lebanese pilot who became the victim of the first Hunter accident when F.6 XG204 hit the ground at high speed three miles from Valley in August 1969. An interval of two years followed before the next fatal crash, which took place in Cwm Penmachno, a sparsely populated valley in Snowdonia.

On Monday, 17 May 1971, during the middle of the afternoon two of 4 FTS' flying instructors, both of whom were highly experienced pilots, climbed into the cockpit of Hunter T.7 XL622 and strapped themselves into their ejection seats. Once the usual cockpit checks had been completed and clearance for take-off obtained, the aircraft taxied along one of the airfield's perimeter tracks before turning on to the runway and lining up for the take-off. Momentarily held on its brakes, while the throttle was opened to full power, the machine accelerated quickly once the brakes were released, and was thrust smoothly by its Rolls-Royce Avon engine into the sky above. After becoming airborne, the T.7 flew towards Snowdonia, where the two instructors intended to practice their low-flying techniques but, sadly, they were destined never to return to Valley, and beyond a few routine radio messages nothing further was heard from them.

At 4.00 p.m. the Hunter was seen entering Cwm Penmachno, which lies some four miles to the east of Blaenau Ffestiniog. Penmachno is a rather isolated valley with a small village located at its head. Some industry, in the form of a slate quarry existed here in the past, but the quarry, like so many others, has long since closed, causing economic decline and depopulation, evident in the run-down condition of many of the village's buildings.

While the aircraft was making progress, flying along the southern side of the valley, it was attracting the attention of a number of people, principally because of the Hunter's unusually low height. Cwm Penmachno's residents saw low flying aircraft frequently (far too frequently some of the villagers would say) and usually not much notice was taken of this aerial activity, except perhaps to grumble about the noise, but on this occasion the jet was so low that people actually stopped what they were doing in order to watch the machine as it moved along, just above the ground.

Among the observers was a farmer driving his tractor in a field. Switching off the tractor's engine so that he could concentrate all the more on the sight before him, he watched with mounting interest, as the Hunter flew, at a height of no more than 100 feet towards the disused quarry at the head of Cwm Penmachno. The farmer assumed the aircraft would soon gain height so that it could leave the valley but contrary to his expectation this did not happen. Instead of climbing, the T.7 started turning to starboard, following the pudding-basin shaped curve of the valley's head, with the intention, it seemed, of continuing along the opposite side of the valley. Whatever the two pilots had in mind, they had performed a most unusual and hazardous manoeuvre. Certainly the watching farmer had never witnessed anything like it previously. Surprised, and not a little apprehensive, he continued to keep the Hunter in sight as it completed its 180° turn but then intervening ground obstructed his line of vision and he lost sight of the jet, which was, in fact, on the very brink of disaster.

Within seconds the farmer heard a loud bang and then saw a cloud of black smoke rising above the hillside, signalling that the aircraft's perilous course had come to an abrupt and violent end. On the valley's northern side there is a succession of small buttresses known as Craig Blaen-y-Cwm and it was one of these, more prominent than the others, into which the T.7 had crashed, at an estimated speed of 200mph.

One man who saw the impact was a Forestry Commission employee, working at that moment in a small plantation of trees adjacent to the derelict quarry. He was concerned about the machine as soon as he saw it approaching: 'I had been watching the plane flying low and in fact had been worried that it was going to crash before it did so,' he said, 'then I saw it hitting a rock, and I should say that if it was fifty or sixty feet higher up, it would have cleared the mountain.' Another person, an Englishman with a holiday cottage in the valley, also watched the Hunter during its final moments: 'After almost completing the turn, the lower wing caught the hillside. Then the plane bounced in the air and completely disintegrated,' he stated. Other witnesses included three women standing in the street outside their homes enjoying a gossip. The jet's presence diverted their attention however, bringing about a halt to the conversation, and then, while looking towards Craig Blaen-y-Cwm the trio were horror-stricken to see the aircraft explode in a ball of fire which threw pieces of burning wreckage far and wide over the hillside.

Other residents of the village, aghast at what had taken place, quickly alerted the emergency services and soon police vehicles, fire engines and ambulances were threading their way, with all the haste they could muster, along the valley's narrow road. Fifty minutes after the crash a helicopter arrived from Valley, followed later by RAF mountain rescue teams. It was nothing less than a full scale turn-out by the emergency services, which in addition to the presence of many sightseers drawn by curiosity, created a stir and bustle not seen for many a year in this isolated community, where little of note seemed to happen. Once at the crash site, rescue parties quickly established that neither of the two pilots had survived — their bodies were found lying, still strapped to their ejection seats, amongst the smouldering wreckage.

But how had the Hunter come to grief? Was the accident simply a result of human misjudgement — outwardly the most obvious cause — or was there technical failure, or a combination of both factors? Many flying accidents are complex events which require a great deal of sleuthing work to unravel what at first appears to be a baffling mystery but in this particular case no such problems existed. Investigators were satisfied that the T.7 was fully serviceable and under control when it hit the ground, and therefore human error was the likeliest, indeed the only explanation for the crash. The rules had plainly been transgressed and with such starkly tragic consequence. Not only had the Hunter descended well below the 250 feet limit allowed for low-level flying but also a risky and unauthorised (we can safely speculate) manoeuvre had been attempted, for which misdemeanour the pilots had paid with their lives.

We can never know which of the two men was flying the jet when it crashed but whichever one had control of the throttle and stick during those final moments before impact, both pilots would of necessity have been concentrating hard on the terrain ahead and keeping a constant look-out for obstacles. Flying at low-level in a hilly area is, by its very nature, a task which demands nothing less than one's total attention, to the exclusion of all else. Three possibilities can be envisaged to explain what took place as the aircraft came out of its turn; a) the pilots saw the protruding buttress in time but then misjudged the avoiding manoeuvre, or b) they did not spot the hazard until it was too late, or c) they failed completely to see the obstruction.

It is, of course, impossible to state with certainty what happened, because there were no survivors, but on balance perhaps b) is the most likely explanation. Probably the two men were looking out well ahead into the turn, a conventional and necessary procedure on their part because anticipation is essential to ensure a clear flight path but in doing so they failed to see, until it was too late, the grave danger which lay much closer. Conventional technique, which in normal circumstances would have ensured their safety, when applied in an unconventional situation merely led to the men's death. Flying at a speed of 200mph so close to the ground meant there was little or no time to correct mistakes — nemesis, swift and brutal, was upon the Hunter and its occupants in an instant.

The air is an unforgiving element and breaking the rules very often carries the severest of penalties for aviators, as demonstrated so well by this accident, which stands as an object lesson in the dangers of low flying.

Chapter 16

'. . . A Catastrophic Loss of Height'

At 7.26 a.m. on Sunday 22 October 1972 a Piper PA30 Twin Comanche, G-AVFV, took off from Southend and headed northwards. The aircraft's destination was RAF Valley, some 250 miles distant. On board the Piper were five people: the 47 year old pilot, his two teenage sons and two family friends, a young married couple, one of whom, the husband, had flying experience and acted as co-pilot during the trip to Anglesey. Prior to the flight, he and his wife had left their baby, only a few months old, in the care of grandparents, but tragically the child would be an orphan before the morning was over. The five were flying to North Wales in order to visit a mutual friend — Mark Ferranti, a member of the well known family of industrialists, who owned a number of properties in the area, as well as a factory at Bangor.

The aircraft was due to arrive at Valley shortly before 10.00 a.m. — a detail of some importance because the pilot had been informed by telephone on the previous day that landings after 10.00 a.m. would not be permitted, it was said, because of the disturbance caused to a local church service. Whether this really was the case or not, the restriction had to be accepted and it became a factor which, as we will see later, strongly influenced the pilot's conduct of the flight during its final stages.

As far as his previous experience was concerned, the pilot's logbook showed that he had held a flying licence (a PPL) since 1963 and had flown for a total of 972 hours. In October 1971 he purchased G-AVFV and at the beginninng of 1972 he received 30 hours of instrument flying training, at the end of which he passed a full instrument rating test. With nearly 1,000 hours accumulated over a period of almost ten years the man's experience was quite extensive, but his familiarity with the demands of instrument flying, after only seven months, was somewhat limited in comparison. Nevertheless, he was qualified to fly under IFR (Instrument Flight Rules) conditions, which happened to prevail during the fatal flight.

Before taking off on that Sunday morning, he and the co-pilot went to the Flight Planning Office at Southend airport but, according to the staff, neither was seen to take note of meteorological charts and data displayed in the office, although the co-pilot did ask for information on Valley's weather. Furthermore, there was no subsequent record of en-route weather information being obtained by the pilots from any other source. Just how much the two men knew about conditions in North Wales is now impossible to establish, but records indicate that the weather was far from ideal; total cloud cover, with the base varying between 1,000 feet and 2,500 feet, outbreaks of light rain or drizzle, and gale force winds blowing from the north west. It was not the most perfect of days to be in the air.

On take-off the aircraft was overloaded by slightly more than 100 lbs, though this had no bearing on the accident because normal fuel consumption would have progressively reduced the weight to well below the authorised maximum of 3,600 lbs. After becoming airborne, the Piper followed an IFR flight plan using airways and flying at an altitude of 8,000 feet until the Wallasey VOR was reached a few minutes before 9.30 a.m., (VORs — Very High Frequency Omnidirectional Ranges — are radio beacons which emit signals that can be used for navigation by aircraft). This part of the flight was accomplished safely.

Then the pilot contacted Preston Air Traffic Control centre and requested either clearance for descent to a lower altitude or for permission to change from IFR to VFR, which meant, if permission was given, descending until free of cloud cover and the ground became visible. Preston responded by clearing the aircraft down to 5,000 feet, a small error on their part, which they quickly rectified by amending the flight level to 5,500 feet — the minimum safe altitude for Valley, because of the mountains on the mainland. Acknowledgement of this information came from the Piper but within minutes its pilot called up the ATC centre once again to ask permission to take a direct route to Valley and leave Airway Blue One, which he had been flying along at this point. Permission was granted, together with a further instruction that the aircraft was to call Valley on the airfield's approach frequency. After little more than a minute had passed, the pilot contacted Preston yet again, this time to request clearance for a descent to 2,500 feet. He was informed that he could do so at his own discretion.

It was 9.41 a.m. when he contacted Valley ATC and gave an Estimated Time of Arrival of 9.50 a.m., to which the controller on duty replied by passing on details of the local weather and giving a course of 270° for the Piper Twin Comanche to steer. The pilot repeated this back to the controller, in accordance with standard procedure, and asked which runway was in use, to be informed that it was Runway 32. He was further requested to call Valley when fifteen miles from the airfield.

Ten minutes later, when, according to its ETA the aircraft should have already landed, its pilot asked for a bearing and was given 310°. At Valley, the radar controller thought this to be rather odd and upon checking his screen saw a contact at a range just short of twenty miles on a bearing of 131°. This combination of direction and distance put the Piper firmly in the region of Snowdon. The alert controller was thus the first person to realise that a potentially dangerous situation was developing. Ascertaining the aircraft's altitude was now a matter of great urgency for him and when he asked for this information the reply was '4,000 feet', which, of course, was an extremely hazardous height to be at in the vicinity of Snowdon, itself only a few hundred feet lower. The pilot was advised by Valley that the minimum safe flight level was 5,500 feet but he appeared not to understand this message and requested that it be repeated. Instead of doing so, however, the controller asked him if he was flying VMC (Visual Meteorological Conditions), which in layman's terms meant could the ground be seen or not? At 4,000 feet the aircraft was totally enveloped by cloud and so the reply was negative. Accordingly, the pilot was instructed to climb to 5,500 feet, which he acknowledged with the words 'Roger, we're climbing to five five.' This was to be his last intelligible message.

One minute later, at 9.52 a.m., another transmission from the Piper Twin Comanche was received but it was so weak and distorted as to be impossible to decipher. Then there was silence.

The scene now moves from the quiet, ordered interior of Valley's air traffic control tower, with its atmosphere of precision and efficiency to a rugged exterior location; the rocky slopes of Snowdon, where gale force winds blew ceaselessly over the rough ground. Perhaps it was not a particularly good day for mountain climbing one might be tempted to observe, but nevertheless many people were out on that misty Sunday morning, determined to be in the hills, come what may.

At the time the Piper was making its final transmission, campers on the shore of Llyn Llydaw, a large lake one mile to the east of Snowdon, heard the sound of an aircraft approaching. It flew over the lake and though unseen by those on the ground because of the cloud, it was obvious the machine was flying at a low altitude. Walkers on the mountain's southern side also heard the aircraft as it drew closer but then, as they listened, the regular beat of engines momentarily faltered before turning into a roar, followed a few seconds later by the unmistakable sounds of an impact.

Visibility was only fifty yards at best, but it did not take long to locate the aircraft, lying on 3,496 feet high Crib-y-Ddysgl, Snowdon's immediate neighbour. Five bodies could be seen among the wreckage. The social call on Mark Ferranti would never be made now. Then there followed the sad task of removing the bodies and informing next-of-kin, always a distressing duty, but especially so in this case because two families had, effectively, been destroyed by the accident.

What had been the sequence of events during the last moments of the flight? An examination of the wreckage indicated the machine was in the act of making a climbing turn to the right, on a heading of 350°, when it struck steep ground on the south east side of Crib-y-Ddysgl some 450 feet below the summit. Both engines were under high power, with the remains of the airspeed indicator showing approximately 130 knots, while the needle of the vertical speed indicator was jammed by impact damage at a reading of 2,000 feet per minute, thus providing clear evidence that the aircraft was attempting to climb at its maximum rate when it hit the ground. Disintegration of the fuselage took place on impact, killing all five occupants instantly. The port wing, after breaking off at the root, had been pushed back into the fuselage, and the other wing, together with the starboard engine, had also become detached and were separated from the main wreckage. Furthest away was the port engine, which had rolled 200 feet down the slope. A post-crash fire occurred in the remains of the cockpit and centre-section which left both burnt out.

But if the machine was flying at 4,000 feet and the throttles were opened to such an extent that a rate of climb of over 2,000 feet per minute was established, how was it that contact with the ground was at an altitude of 3,040 feet, some 1,000 feet *below* the height at which the Piper was presumed to be flying?

One explanation could be incorrect altimeter settings causing the two instruments installed in the aircraft to indicate more height than was the case in reality. Accident investigators removed both altimeters from the wreckage and discovered one was set to 1026 mb while the other showed 1029 mb. These settings were thought to be reliable to within plus or minus 2 mb, and so it is probable that G-AVFV was indeed flying at the height which had been reported to Valley. So how had the aircraft lost so much altitude when it was supposed to be climbing fast? The answer was to be found in the fact that a gale force wind was blowing that Sunday morning, the result of which was to cause severe downcurrents of air over high ground.

The effect of strong winds in mountainous regions had already been studied by the Meteorological Office and reported in the publication *Airflow over Mountains*, (MO 621B), from which the following extract is quoted:

> 'Most hilly regions contain long ridges of high ground
> or a series of individual features which together make
> up what are effectively ridges. If the wind is flowing
> transversely across such a ridge it is important to realise
> that an aircraft flying more or less parallel to it might
> remain in a down current continuously until the whole
> length of the ridge has been traversed. In such
> circumstances *catastrophic loss of height could occur*.'

[author's italics]

Crib-y-Ddysgl, as part of the Snowdon complex, takes the form of a curved ridge whose axis lies roughly in a south-west to north-east direction and as the gale on 22 October was blowing from the north-west it would be at right angles to the ridge, thereby creating severe downcurrents and turbulence to the south-east of the mountain which, literally, brought about the downfall of the Piper Twin Comanche. Despite the power of its two Lycoming engines at full throttle, the aircraft could not overcome the enormous pressure exerted by rapidly moving downcurrents of air. A brief but unequal struggle ensued between the blind, unrelenting forces of Nature and a machine devised by men, the outcome of which contest was inevitable. Pitted against the elemental strength of the wind, the Piper had little chance of escaping from the trap which had fatally ensnared it.

But how did the aircraft come to be in an area which it should patently have avoided at all costs? One thing is clear from the outset; the pilot did not intentionally fly so close to the mountains. It is more than likely he was not aware of his exact position until shortly before the accident, and once he realised the gravity of the situation, he immediately attempted to extricate himself and his luckless passengers from the terrible danger which they faced. Probably it was the pilot's desire to arrive at Valley before the 10.00 a.m. deadline, which the RAF authorities stipulated had to be strictly adhered to, that prompted him to depart from the planned track, but in doing so he seems to have made insufficient allowance for the strong winds blowing at the time.

Of significance also is the fact that during the flight to Wallasey the aircraft arrived over each airway reporting point a few minutes after the estimated time, proving that not enough allowance was made for the strong headwinds being encountered. After passing over Wallasey, the Piper flew westwards for fourteen minutes and at 9.40 a.m., when its pilot first contacted Valley, the aircraft's position, according to calculations made after the accident, was one mile north of Colwyn Bay. To fly from this point to Valley in the prevailing weather conditions would have taken eighteen minutes but when the pilot, at 9.41 a.m., gave an ETA of 9.50 a.m. (i.e. only nine minutes flying time) he must, therefore, have believed himself to be nearer his destination than was actually the case.

His next action was to change course by turning 45° to port and flying on a south westerly heading for 25 miles until the aircraft was at a point close to cloud obscured Snowdon. This part of the flight took nine minutes, at the end of which, it will be remembered, messages passed between Valley and the Piper, as a consequence of which its pilot was instructed to turn on to a heading of 310° and climb immediately. He responded to this request without hesitation and initiated a steep climbing turn to the right. This manoeuvre took G-AVFV into the lee of Snowdon, where the aircraft, in the words of the accident investigators: 'was subjected to sustained downcurrents of exceptional severity which resulted in a catastrophic loss of height.'

There remains one question outstanding; why did the pilot turn inland at Colwyn Bay? The most likely explanation, already alluded to, is that he believed he was at a point much further along his intended track. He probably thought that he was at the north eastern end of the Menai Strait and the turn was carried out in order to position the aircraft for an approach to Valley which would ensure arrival before the 10.00 a.m. deadline.

During the final minutes of the flight the pilot gave no indication that he was encumbered by any problems but it is likely, in the seconds immediately preceding the crash, that severe turbulence would have caused control difficulty. Perhaps this is what he was attempting to communicate in his final, distorted message. This distortion was probably caused by the fact that the Piper, at the moment of transmission, was below the summit of Crib-y-Ddysgl and the mountain's bulk acted as a shield preventing the efficient reception at Valley of signals from the aircraft's radio.

Investigators concluded that the crash was caused by navigational error — primarily a failure to appreciate the strength of the north westerly wind and to make the necessary allowance for drift, in consequence of which the aircraft, after passing Wallasey, was flying well to the south of its intended track. The accident illustrates how a number of factors, often unrelated and innocent enough in themselves, can work in combination to bring about disaster; in this case, the pilot's lack of appreciation of the wind's strength, the imposition of a deadline by Valley which in turn imparted a sense of urgency to the flight in its latter stages, the pilot's attempt at what was essentially a short cut to save time, and the total cloud cover over the region which prevented any visual check on progress and position. Perhaps if there was no deadline to meet or an occasional gap had appeared in the unbroken cloud then the outcome of the flight might well have been different.

Powerful downcurrents of air are a permanent hazard of flying close to mountains and frequently present an invisible trap for the unwary. In recent years there have been some narrow escapes, one notable example being the case of Piper Cherokee G-AVWG. On Sunday 11 December 1988 this aircraft was on a flight from Blackpool airport to Mona, in Anglesey. Aboard the Cherokee were four people: the pilot — a Lancashire businessman — and three of his friends, all Canadians.

Their trip was something of a sight-seeing one because after flying over Conwy so that the Canadians could observe the ancient town and its castle, G-AVWG headed west to allow the passengers an aerial view of the Conwy Valley and nearby hills. But on approaching the eastern side of Tal-y-Fan the pilot suddenly found himself in serious trouble; the Cherokee was caught in a strong downcurrent. Enjoyment of the mountains and their scenic splendours rapidly dissolved into stomach churning anxiety as the aircraft was dragged inexorably towards the ground. There was to be no escape, as the pilot himself commented: 'We just seemed to lose power and couldn't get a climb going. This was at about 2,000 feet and I realised we wouldn't clear the hillside. So I put out a May Day and made sure the passengers were strapped in safely.'

'Once we were committed I had only ten seconds to make up my mind and make for a spot between the rocks which was as safe as possible to put the plane down. I kept raising the nose and I suppose when we touched the ground we were about to stall. I had a second to dodge the sheep and a couple of rocks, and I managed to land uphill in a sort of belly-flop.' In fact, it was an excellent landing, considering the difficulty. The pilot had succeeded in retaining some control over his aircraft and managed to put the machine down on the most uninviting piece of ground imaginable for a forced landing — rough, broken hillside with liberal scatterings of rocks and gorse bushes.

This was not the first aircraft to come to grief on this part of Tal-y-Fan however. Back in August 1942 a Blackburn Botha from RAF Squires Gate, Blackpool (which became the town's airport and the very one from which G-AVWG had taken off) crashed at a spot within hailing distance of where the Cherokee now lay, but in the case of the wartime accident there were no survivors.

Though the Cherokee's pilot could be criticised for failing to appreciate the risk of downcurrents he, nevertheless, displayed admirable flying skills once the danger became a reality. By getting the aircraft on to the ground, more or less in one piece, he undoubtedly saved his life and the lives of his three passengers. Instead of dead bodies on the mountainside, there were four lucky people — slightly shaken perhaps, but at least they were alive. The passengers' comments reveal their gratitude: 'We're lucky to be alive. The pilot did a great job.' . . . 'The pilot was marvellous.' . . . 'We had a lucky escape — that pilot is the greatest.' After being taken to Conwy police station, where they recovered from their misadventure, the four flyers returned to Lancashire — by road.

As the Cherokee belonged to Blackpool Aero Club, it was they who faced the problem of recovering the machine from its present, forlorn position on the hillside. On the day after the accident, the Club's chief engineer and two assistants travelled to Conwy, where they booked in to a hotel before continuing to Tal-y-Fan in order to make an inspection of the crash-landing site and assess how best to remove the aircraft. Dismantling was the obvious (indeed the only) solution, and so, early on the morning of Tuesday 13 December the three men drove in a hired truck up the steep, narrow lanes which lead from the lush meadows of the Conwy Valley to the bleak hill slopes high above, shrouded that day in the Stygian gloom of a mountain mist so impenetrably thick and murky as to be almost beyond description.

The truck, which would be used to transport the dismantled Cherokee, was driven as close as possible to the aircraft's location but it was still three quarters of a mile away across ground which the lorry could not negotiate with safety and so a local farmer obligingly offered the use of his tractor and trailer for the final part of the journey. Luckily there was a track, of sorts, which led to a disused quarry and which the tractor was able to traverse without much difficulty. The Cherokee lay within a few yards of this track. By lunchtime, with the mist as dense as ever, the job of dismantling was complete and the machine's fuselage, wings and tailplane had been taken to the waiting wagon. Prior to transportation back to Blackpool, all the aircraft's remaining fuel, amounting to twenty gallons, was siphoned out and offered to the farmer, who gleefully accepted this surprise gift!

The most recent example of the 'downcurrent' type of mishap in Snowdonia was on 12 June 1991, when an Enstrom F-28C helicopter (G-BGSN) was engaged on filming work in the area of Marchlyn Mawr lake, on the north eastern side of Elidir Fawr. Marchlyn, once an unspoilt and secluded stretch of water, is now part of the National Grid's pumped storage hydroelectric power station at Dinorwig. A Nottingham based film production team was making a recruitment video for the construction industry and had hired a helicopter to film some aerial sequences above the lake. On board the Enstrom was the pilot and a cameraman, while other members of the production team stood by the water's edge. The weather was dry but dull, with a strong wind blowing from the south west. At RAF Valley the mean wind speed that day was 22 knots with gale force gusts of 40 knots also recorded. In the mountains, these conditions would have created disturbed, swirling air currents of great force. Many aviators might have concluded that it was imprudent to fly a light helicopter in this hilly area on such a windy day because of the danger from downcurrents, but it was a risk ignored by the team, possibly because of commercial considerations and a desire to complete the filming.

Shortly before 11.00 a.m., as the Enstrom flew above the dark waters of Marchlyn a fierce gust seized the machine and pushed it relentlessly downwards with a power graphically described by one eye-witness as being 'Like Monty Python's boot!' However, the pilot skilfully managed to cushion the helicopter's impact as it hit the water and both he and the cameraman escaped unhurt. They began swimming to the shore, only fifty yards away, while the Enstrom quickly sank into the depths. This event caused a temporary halt in electricity production at the power station, though it was only a precautionary measure in case any wreckage should find its way into the system of water pipes and cause damage. On the following day any such risk was eliminated by the prompt and efficient recovery of the wrecked helicopter.

When a newspaper reporter asked a pertinent question regarding the suitability of flying conditions, the film team's leader replied, somewhat defensively: 'It would be wonderful if we were all blessed with hindsight. We had no reason to believe that was going to happen . . . it was a freak gust.' The truth, however, was that taking to the air on that windy day was not the simple and straightforward matter it would have been in calmer conditions; the danger was greater than normal and the flight was, in reality, something of a gamble which did not come off. Every flying accident contains a lesson in air safety, which in this particular case happens to be clear and unequivocal; never underestimate the hazardous combination of strong winds and high ground. Their unwitting conspiracy creates a natural power whose disregard by a pilot can so easily prove fatal.

Bibliography

Alexander, Raymond, *101 Squadron*, published privately by the author, 1979.

Card, Frank, *Whensoever* (The Ernest Press, 1993)
50 years of the RAF Mountain Rescue Service 1943-1993

Doylerush, Edward, *No Landing Place* (Midland Counties Publications, 1985).

Doylerush, Edward, *Fallen Eagles* (Midland Counties Publications, 1990).

Loraine, Winifred, *Robert Loraine, Soldier, Actor, Airman* (Collins, 1938).
An excellent biography written by Loraine's wife.

Moffatt, Gwen, *Two Star Red* (Hodder & Stoughton, 1964).
A book about RAF Mountain Rescue.

O'Sullivan, Richard W., *An Irishman's Aviation Sketchbook* (Irish Aviator, 1988).
Includes an account of the investigation into the crash of an Aer Lingus Dakota in Snowdonia, January 1952.

Sloan, Roy, *Early Aviation in North Wales* (Gwasg Carreg Gwalch, 1989).
Sloan, Roy, *Wings of War over Gwynedd* (Gwasg Carreg Gwalch, 1991).
History of aviation in Gwynedd during World War II.

Smith, David J., *Action Stations, 3. Military Airfields in Wales and the North West* (Patrick Stephens Ltd., 1981).

Smith, David J., *High Ground Wrecks, 3rd Edition* (Midland Counties Publications, 1989).

Snowdonia Aviation Historical Group, *The Air War over Gwynedd, 1985.*
Booklet containing brief descriptions of 35 wartime crashes.

Wales, Eighth Air Force Research Group, *Pieces of Eight*, official journal, Volume 1, No. 5.